SAINT PAUL

SAINT✝PAUL
CALLED TO CONVERSION

a
seven-day
retreat

RONALD D. WITHERUP, s.s.

ST. ANTHONY MESSENGER PRESS
Cincinnati, Ohio

Cover and book design by Mark Sullivan
Cover image:
Batoni, Pompeo (1708–1787), Portrait of St. Paul.
Basildon Park, Berkshire, Great Britain
Photo Credit: National Trust / Art Resource, NY

LIBRARY OF CONGRESS CATALOGING-IN-PUBLICATION DATA

Witherup, Ronald D., 1950-
Saint Paul : called to conversion a seven-day retreat / Ronald D. Witherup.
p. cm.
Includes bibliographical references.
ISBN 978-0-86716-529-6 (pbk. : alk. paper) 1. Spiritual retreats—Catholic Church. 2. Paul, the Apostle, Saint. 3. Spirituality—Catholic Church. I. Title.

BX2376.5.W58 2007
269'.6—dc22

2007008746

ISBN 978-0-86716-529-6

Published by St. Anthony Messenger Press
28 W. Liberty St.
Cincinnati, OH 45202
www.SAMPBooks.org

Printed in the United States of America.

Printed on acid-free paper.

08 09 10 11 5 4 3 2

CONTENTS

INTRODUCING
PAUL
THE
APOSTLE

SAINT PAUL IS THE MOST PROMINENT PERSONALITY OF the New Testament, apart from Jesus himself. Thirteen of the twenty-seven books of the New Testament bear his name. All of them are letters. Much of what we know about Paul comes from these remarkable written sources, supplemented by stories from the Acts of the Apostles, in which Paul figures prominently in the second half (chapters 9–28). These are the only two sources for Paul's life; however, they differ at times in details. Lacking any formal biography, biblical scholars have been able to piece together the basic outline of Paul's life. They use Paul's letters as the primary source of information, since they are first–person accounts. Acts is used to complement and supplement that information.

Paul (also known by his Jewish name Saul[1]) was born in Tarsus, Cilicia, in Asia Minor (now modern-day Turkey) probably between AD 1 and 10.[2] He was a diaspora Jew, that is, a Jew living outside the homeland of Palestine. Tarsus was a large, prosperous city in the Roman Empire, so it is quite fair to call Paul an urbanite. He was likely well educated, apparently a student of the great rabbi Gamaliel I in Jerusalem (ca. AD 20–50).[3]

Paul himself admits that he persecuted the church out of zeal for his Jewish background.[4] However, around the year AD 35 he had a remarkable experience on the road to Damascus in which the risen Lord Jesus appeared to him and called him to be "the apostle to the Gentiles."[5] Paul never describes this event in detail. Rather, he speaks of a "revelation of Jesus Christ"[6] that leaves the impression of a supernatural appearance of the resurrected Jesus, or perhaps what we might call a mystical experience. Paul would not characterize his experience as a "conversion" in the sense of a change of religion, but more likely as a "call" or "commission." Acts portrays the event in terms reminiscent of the call of Old Testament prophets, and this is consistent with Paul's own view. Paul considers himself an "apostle," one who has been called and sent by the Lord Jesus himself for a special mission. He was to bring the gentiles into the fold of those who accepted Jesus of Nazareth as the long-awaited Messiah and Savior of the world.

After his call, Paul began an intense ministry of evangelization. He took up (or returned to) the work of tent making so that he would not be a burden to the communities he served.[7] After a mysterious three-year period in Arabia,[8] he went to Jerusalem to meet with Peter, James, the brother of the Lord, and John (ca. AD 38). They were leaders of the new movement of Jesus' followers in Jerusalem that Acts calls "the Way"[9] and who eventually became known as "Christians."[10] These leaders apparently endorsed Paul's mission to the gentiles. Paul, accompanied by colleagues, then went to Syria, Cilicia and Galatia and eventually crossed over into Europe to proclaim the gospel of Jesus Christ in Macedonia, Achaia and throughout the Mediterranean region. This period of Paul's journeys can be dated from AD 38 to 50.

Acts portrays Paul's missionary activity in a series of three journeys. While there can be no doubt that Paul's travels were extensive, the portrait in Acts may be somewhat artificial. It corresponds roughly to the geographical outlook of Acts 1:8, which shows the expanding Christian mission in stages, going from Judea to Samaria to "the ends of the earth." In any case, Paul's ministry was missionary evangelization, which he exercised with great effect. He established communities of faith in many major cities of the Roman Empire, such as Ephesus, Corinth, Philippi and Thessalonica.

In the last decade or more of his life, Paul not only continued his missionary activity but also wrote letters (ca. AD 50–60). The letters that survive in our New Testament, in their canonical order, are: Romans, 1 and 2 Corinthians, Galatians, Ephesians, Philippians, Colossians, 1 and 2 Thessalonians, 1 and 2 Timothy, Titus and Philemon.[11] Letters afforded him an excellent means to stay in touch with the communities that he founded on his various missions. His disciples preserved them for later Christians, assembling them into a collection that formed the foundations for the New Testament. At times, Paul would write from prison, one of the many different experiences of suffering he endured as a follower of Jesus. At other times he would write to admonish his communities, to instruct them, to encourage them and to express his plans for the future. On at least one occasion, the Letter to the Romans, he wrote to introduce himself to a community that had been founded by others. The earliest letter of Paul is 1 Thessalonians (AD 50–51); the last letter is either Romans or Philemon (ca. AD 58–60).

Although the New Testament never describes it, ancient tradition says that Paul was martyred during imprisonment in Rome, probably around AD 62–64. Many paintings of the apostle portray him with a sword at hand, symbolizing the likelihood that he was beheaded during the persecutions conducted by the Roman emperor Nero (AD 54–68).

By any estimation, Paul was a formidable personality. He argued persuasively with the well-known early Christian leaders, especially Peter and James, over the need to adapt the gospel of Jesus Christ to the gentiles.[12] He also had no trouble sternly reprimanding his communities whenever he thought they had strayed from the gospel he preached.[13] But he also loved his communities dearly and treated them as good parents treat their children.[14] At one point he compares himself to a nursing mother: "But we were gentle among you, like a nurse tenderly caring for her own children."[15] Elsewhere he calls himself their "father."[16] This balanced combination of discipline and affection makes Paul a good candidate to be an effective retreat master.

More importantly, Paul's letters contain tremendous insights into the spiritual life. Paul explicitly desired that his communities become "holy." He tells the Thessalonians outright, "For this is the will of God, your sanctification."[17] And he reminds the Ephesians that they are "to clothe yourselves with the new self, created according to the likeness of God in true righteousness and holiness."[18] Holiness is our destiny as

Christians. Like all Jews of his day, Paul's understanding of holiness was not something people could accomplish on their own. Rather, holiness meant becoming more and more God-like. Christians inherited this perspective. God is the only truly holy one. Our sanctity is merely derivative of God's essence, and true holiness only comes about by surrendering ourselves to God's will and God's power. On our retreat, we will remain conscious of this goal and invite Paul's assistance in this process.

PAUL'S WORLD

Identifying with Paul's world should not to be too difficult for us who live in the twenty-first century. Despite the centuries that separate us, Paul's world, in some ways, resembles our own. It was quite diverse, multicultural and multilingual. There were complex secular trends and diverse religious beliefs that made for a challenging context in which to proclaim the message of Jesus Christ. Like our own time, there were also many sharp divisions in Paul's world. Promoting a harmonious, common identity was no easy chore. In short, there were many different influences on Paul, and it is good for us to take them into account before we delve into his spiritual teachings. Most importantly, we need to look briefly at three primary influences: Judaism, Hellenism and the Roman Empire.

The Influence of Judaism

Like Jesus, Paul was born a Jew and lived his entire life as a Jew. He was quite proud of his Jewish heritage. In Philippians he summarizes his background thus:

circumcised on the eighth day, a member of the people of Israel, of the tribe of Benjamin, a Hebrew born of Hebrews; as to the law, a Pharisee; as to zeal, a persecutor of the church; as to righteousness under the law, blameless.[19]

Despite his call to follow Jesus, which we often characterize as his "conversion," he never claims to have abandoned Judaism. Note that he highlights his Pharisaic background. That may surprise us, who want to be directed on this retreat. We may think of the Pharisees as the enemies of Jesus, and therefore our enemies.[20] While it is true that some Pharisees and other Jewish leaders strongly opposed Jesus and plotted against him, not all Pharisees acted in this way. They did, however, largely oppose the early Christians. They were zealous for their Jewish religious heritage. Paul admits this of himself and even boasts of it. Once he accepted the risen Jesus as Lord, however, all that changed. As he says in Philippians:

I regard everything as loss because of the surpassing value of knowing Christ Jesus my Lord. For his sake I have suffered the loss of all things, and I regard them as rubbish, in order that I may gain Christ.[21]

This is Paul's way of asserting the supreme importance of his newfound faith.

I think the zeal that so characterized his life as a Pharisee shifted in him when he was called by Jesus Christ to be the apostle to the gentiles. His zeal transferred to his faith in Christ. Nothing else mattered. But nowhere in his letters does he use the term "Christian" to refer to himself or to any members of his communities. Rather, he uses the term "the saints" to describe the followers of Jesus—those who are called to holiness in communion with Christ.[22] The root idea of the word "saint" is actually someone called and set apart for a special mission. That is the way Paul envisioned this new community of faith.

We also need to remember the complexity of the first-century Judaism that Paul knew. It was not a uniform, monolithic faith. There were multiple divisions within Judaism. Four types of Jewish perspective are especially prominent.

The first is Palestinian Judaism. It existed in Palestine, that is, Judea and Galilee, in what Christians now call the Holy Land. Some of its characteristics included worship centered around the temple in Jerusalem and its priesthood, and the various cultic rituals that were a part of the routine regimen of piety. Even this type of Judaism was not uniform. Some who thought the purity of their faith was being threatened by the compromises of their religious leaders fled to the Dead Sea and established a kind of ascetical community at Qumran. Their desire was to escape the bad influence of the secular world and thus preserve authentic faith. (Some fundamentalist Christians today have reacted to modern life in like fashion and try to separate themselves completely from modern secular influences.)

A second type of Judaism is called Hellenistic Judaism. This was, in fact, Paul's primary background, since he was born and raised outside of Palestine. The word "Hellenistic" means Greek. It refers to the Greek culture that was the primary cultural influence in Paul's day, dating from the time of Alexander the Great (333 BC). Once the Jews were dispersed throughout the world after the first destruction of Jerusalem (by the Babylonians in 587 BC), they settled in many foreign lands. They adapted so much to their new surroundings that many of them eventually lost command of their native Aramaic and Hebrew languages. They gradually translated their holy writings, which eventually became the Hebrew Bible (what we know as the Old Testament), into Greek, the language of the ruling empire. This translation is called the Septuagint, from the Roman numeral for seventy (LXX), symbolizing the seventy scribes who legend says accomplished the translation in seventy days and nights. This text enabled the Jews in the diaspora to preserve, but also to adapt, their faith. Paul no doubt used the Septuagint, as his letters show familiarity with it when quoting from or alluding to the Old Testament.

Rabbinic Judaism is the third type. Its roots are obscure but go back to some two hundred years before Paul. Its name derives from the "rabbis," the Jewish leaders who particularly rose to prominence after the second destruction of Jerusalem (by the Romans in AD 70). In the wake of this traumatic destruction, certain Jewish leaders of Pharisaic background adapted Judaism, collecting and preserving their sacred writings, and finally incorporating them into a permanent sacred canon, the Hebrew Bible. The rabbis' timeless interpretation and adaptation of the Old Testament, in particular, influenced Paul's own approach to these sacred texts. Paul shows himself to be adept at rabbinic interpretation of texts in new circumstances. In fact, we could well consider Paul a "rabbi" in the sense of his teaching and preaching style.[23]

The fourth Jewish influence is apocalyptic Judaism. It is expressed in a type of literature found in the Old Testament called "apocalyptic." The word literally means "unveiling." It refers to an outlook that envisions the revelation of God's victory over evil at the end of time. The book of Daniel is a prime example of this kind of literature. In the New Testament, the book of Revelation is an example. Apocalyptic literature springs from the experience of dire persecution. It expresses a dualistic outlook of a cosmic battle between good and evil, God and the devil, light and darkness and so on. This perspective developed several hundred years before Jesus and Paul, but it continued to exercise considerable influence in their times. Ultimately, its message is a hopeful one: Despite appearances in the world around us, God and the forces of good will win the final battle. There will be a judgment day, and all wrongs will be righted. The good will be rewarded and the bad properly punished.

Paul inherited aspects of this worldview that is also found in certain teachings of Jesus in the Gospels.[24] Sometimes, Paul seems quite taken with this perspective and urges people to prepare for an imminent end of the world.[25] It also influenced his ethical teachings sometimes. The point is that we should be aware of this apocalyptic perspective when we read his letters, because it is not exactly our own. Now, some two thousand years removed from Paul's teaching, we realize that we do not know God's timetable for bringing this world to its judgment day. The end is not as imminent as it was for Paul. Periodically, such as when the year 2000 rolled around, some people resurrect this apocalyptic outlook and call people to repent, for "the end of the world is near." While the message is still a valid one, the timetable is not. We do not have the apocalyptic urgency that Paul sometimes expresses in his letters. It is one of those Jewish influences that were part of Paul's world and that carried over into later Christian teaching.

The Influence of Hellenism

We have already said that Hellenism is the Greek cultural influence that reigned in Paul's day. This influence was wide-ranging. It might be compared with the tremendous influence of English and American capitalism in our own day. Almost anywhere you go in the world today, someone there can usually speak English. Along with that goes the influence of American culture (McDonald's, Coca-Cola and Hollywood movies seem to be everywhere!), which other nationalities do not always appreciate. As with any culture, such influence can be controversial.

In Paul's day Koine (common) Greek was the main language, and he was obviously conversant in it. He wrote all his letters in this type of Greek. Along with language came the impact of Greek culture on daily life. Social and political institutions derived from Greek culture. Examples abound. For instance, the notion of the city-state and the importance of being a citizen of such a community likely influenced Paul's language regarding the "body of Christ." The gymnasium as a center for athletic contests and social interchange was another prominent Hellenistic institution. Paul is familiar with these activities. Maybe we could think of Paul as an ancient sports fan. He uses considerable sports imagery in his letters (boxing, running the race, wrestling) to illustrate his message.[26]

Another example was the wide appeal among the general public of various philosophies that flourished in the Hellenistic world, such as Cynicism, Stoicism and Epicureanism. The Cynics favored a return to "the natural life" and advocated living ascetically. They despised hucksters who fed off the rich, and they taught the importance of working for a living. The Stoics, who derived their thought from Cynic philosophy, emphasized self-sufficiency and keeping control over one's emotions, especially in the face of life's difficulties. Finally, the Epicureans sought pleasure as the supreme value in life but lived in a balanced and peaceful manner. These philosophies and others exercised considerable influence in Paul's day. Paul himself adopted some of their techniques, such as working for his own living. Many people were attracted to these philosophical schools to help them address life's problems. They provide a backdrop for some of Paul's ethical and theological concerns.

Yet another influence was in the religious sphere. The Hellenistic world fostered an attraction to many different cults dedicated to pagan gods and goddesses, such as Isis and Artemis.[27] Paul clearly opposed such influences by emphasizing monotheism, the belief in one God characteristic of Jewish faith, and what God had done in Jesus Christ to save the world.

In short, Hellenistic language and culture had a huge impact on life in Paul's day, whether for good or for ill, and his letters often reflect this background.

The Influence of the Roman Empire

Finally, we cannot ignore the influence of the Roman Empire in Paul's world. Rome was the ruling world power in the West. (Remember that inhabitants of Paul's world were less aware at the time of such tremendous cultures as India and China in the East.) Paul himself was a Roman citizen.

Rome's power was felt in numerous ways. Most importantly, the world was basically at peace. The *Pax Romana* (Latin for "Roman peace") meant that travel on the extensive Roman road system and in sleek ships was fairly safe from threat of criminal attack, though still always hazardous. Paul took advantage of this relative calm, utilizing this Roman transportation system when he went on his extensive apostolic journeys to preach the gospel. He went all over the eastern Mediterranean world, journeyed to Rome itself, and planned to go to Spain, to the far western reaches of the empire, before he was martyred.[28] Paul also uses his Roman citizenship to ensure a fair legal proceeding.[29] Rome retained the ultimate political authority over life and death. Rome, then, was always in the background, a power that could not be ignored.

Paul, like all of us, was a product of his era. To some degree, he believed that many influences in the surrounding culture were detrimental to the spiritual health of his communities. In other instances, Paul knew how to use common cultural images to good effect in order to get his message across to his audience. As we prepare to employ his letters to guide us on this retreat, we keep in mind this dual appreciation of culture.

Notes
1. See Acts 13:9.
2. See Acts 9:11; 22:3.
3. See Acts 22:3.
4. Philippians 3:6; cf. Acts 9:1.
5. Acts 9:1–19; cf. Romans 11:13.
6. Galatians 1:12.
7. Acts 18:3; 1 Thessalonians 2:9.
8. Galatians 1:17. Scholars speculate that Paul might have received instruction about the faith or the stories of Jesus from other Christians during this time.
9. Acts 9:2; 19:23; 22:4.

10. Acts 11:26.
11. Biblical scholars suggest that only seven of the thirteen letters of Paul are without dispute from Paul's own hand (Romans, 1 and 2 Corinthians, Galatians, Philippians, 1 Thessalonians and Philemon). The remaining six are disputed in authorship. They are designated Deutero-Pauline, meaning that they were possibly composed by later anonymous authors at a different time, most likely disciples or companions of Paul. For our purposes on this retreat, all thirteen letters provide a good source of Paul's spiritual vision. There were also other letters that have apparently been lost. For example, Paul refers to other letters of his (1 Corinthians 5:9; 2 Corinthians 7:8) and mentions one from the Laodiceans (Colossians 4:16). Moreover, a complex letter like 2 Corinthians most likely consists of fragments of multiple letters addressed to that community and that have not been preserved whole. For more information, see Ronald D. Witherup, *101 Questions and Answers on Paul* (Mahwah, N.J.: Paulist, 2003), pp. 12–14, 86–90.
12. Galatians 2:11–14.
13. Galatians 1:6–9; 1 Corinthians 5:1–2.
14. 1 Thessalonians 2:11.
15. 1 Thessalonians 2:7b.
16. 1 Corinthians 4:15; 1 Thessalonians 2:11; Philemon 10.
17. 1 Thessalonians 4:3a. The words *sanctification* and *holiness* are interchangeable.
18. Ephesians 4:24.
19. Philippians 3:5–6; cf. Acts 21:39. In a more polemical passage, he also draws attention to his Jewish heritage to defend his apostolic call (2 Corinthians 11:22).
20. The Gospels' strong condemnation of the Pharisees reflects the later situation that developed after Jesus' death and resurrection, when sharp divisions began to appear between those Jews who accepted Jesus as Messiah and those who did not.
21. Philippians 3:8.
22. Romans 1:7; 1 Corinthians 1:2; Philippians 1:1.
23. One recent book takes this idea seriously and makes for interesting reading. See Bruce Chilton, *Rabbi Paul: An Intellectual Biography* (New York: Doubleday, 2004). Remember that "rabbi" was a title also used of Jesus (Mark 9:5; 11:21).
24. See, for example, Mark 13:1–37 or Matthew 24:3–28.

25. See 1 Thessalonians 4:13—5:11.
26. 1 Corinthians 9:24‒27; Galatians 2:2; Colossians 4:12.
27. See Acts 19:21‒41.
28. See Romans 15:24, 28.
29. Acts 22:25‒27.

DAY ONE

PAUL MIGHT SEEM, AT FIRST GLANCE, AN ODD CHOICE FOR A retreat director. Already in the New Testament, some readers recognized that his writings could be confusing and perhaps misleading. One author warns:

> So also our beloved brother Paul wrote to you according to the wisdom given him, speaking of this as he does in all his letters. There are some things in them hard to understand, which the ignorant and unstable twist to their own destruction, as they do the other scriptures. You therefore, beloved, since you are forewarned, beware that you are not carried away with the error of the lawless and lose your own stability.[1]

This sentiment from another New Testament author seems almost as if Paul's letters should come with a warning label:

"Use With Caution: Contents May Be Hazardous to Your Spiritual Health."

This probably should not surprise us. Paul, after all, has been the focus of many different debates throughout Christian history. One notable figure from the second century, Marcion, a leader in the church at Rome who unfortunately became a heretic, tried to make Paul the centerpiece of the New Testament canon. He thought Paul alone, along with Luke (as evidenced in his Gospel), understood the truth of God's message, so he rejected the Old Testament and the other three Gospels. In the end, the church judged Marcion's viewpoint to be too restrictive.

From the fourth century, Saint John Chrysostom provides a model for proper appreciation of Paul and his letters. He wrote many commentaries on Paul's writings. Reflecting on the use of Paul's letters in liturgy, he writes:

> As I keep hearing the Epistles of blessed Paul read, and that twice every week, and often three or four times, whenever we are celebrating the memorials of the holy martyrs, gladly do I enjoy the spiritual trumpet, and get roused and warmed with desire at recognizing the voice so dear to me, and seem to fancy him all but present to my sight, and behold him conversing with me.[2]

Chrysostom's only regret was that not everyone in his day seemed to appreciate the apostle as well as he did. This is one indication that Paul's letters were not uniformly honored or well-known in Chrysostom's day.

The Protestant Reformation in the sixteenth century provides another example. Paul's notion of justification by faith alone, in fact, was one of the primary underpinnings of the

Reformation. Martin Luther's reading of the Letter to the Romans led him to question many practices of the Roman Catholic church in his day. Today Catholics have had to admit that Luther had a good point, even if he took it to extremes. The church needed to be reformed, and Paul was a good resource to help accomplish the job. Unfortunately, the reforms got way out of control and caused one of the most destructive schisms in Christian history, the impact of which is still felt in our day.

Fortunately, though, by means of a formal statement between Roman Catholics and the major Lutheran churches, there is now more agreement than disagreement over what Paul meant by his important concept of justification by faith, which we will discuss on Day Two.[3] Remarkably, because of this statement, more than four hundred years of Christian division and strife have been overcome, at least in part. Even more amazing is that this new understanding and common appreciation of Paul's teaching has been reached only four decades after the end of the Second Vatican Council (1962–1965), which fostered fervent ecumenical discussions.

Controversial as Paul has been, all Christians recognize that his letters are deeply spiritual. It is true that anyone can misread Scripture. Paul's letters are no exception in this regard. (People have been misinterpreting the book of Revelation for ages, applying it literally as a blueprint to various scenarios of the cataclysmic end of the world. Reading it this way doesn't make it necessarily so.) As the author of 2 Peter suggests, Paul's letters can be applied wrongly, too. But read in their proper context, they can provide a wonderful road map for a spiritual journey on a retreat.

OUR RETREAT DIRECTOR

I have another reason for wanting to propose Paul as a retreat director. In my experience, many Catholics do not know Paul well. We gravitate toward the Gospel stories of Jesus or the stories of the early church in Acts more frequently for our preaching and teaching, and we seldom concentrate on the New Testament letters. This is quite understandable. The Gospels are about Jesus, and the Acts of the Apostles is about the church. Stories and parables are naturally more attractive than letters. Moreover, many people find Paul hard to understand. He can come across as too philosophical, too abstract. I hope that this book might make a small contribution in turning people, especially Catholics, back to Paul and his letters. There is a rich spiritual tradition there that should not be lost.

Why do I think that Paul makes an excellent retreat director? For one thing, he comes across in his letters as a real human being. He had his struggles, his limitations and his faults, but he also touched on the most sublime of spiritual truths. He could be bold and demanding, but he could also be gentle and supportive. Parts of his letters can send readers into spiritual ecstasy. Indeed, at times I think he himself experienced such deeply spiritual insight on more than one occasion, while dictating his letters or while undergoing the most challenging trials, such as persecution, rejection and betrayal on the part of companions or some of his beloved communities. Paul's own firm faith and confident hope and consistent prayer life shine through in such circumstances.

Some might still be a little wary of placing themselves in the hands of such a saint. He can seem a little volatile. To help allay such fears, I would like to recall a portrait of Saint Paul by the renowned Dutch painter, Rembrandt van Rijn (1606–1669). In 2005 the National Gallery of Art in Washington, D.C., held a special exhibit of many of Rembrandt's late religious works of art. A centerpiece of the exhibition was his "Self-Portrait as the Apostle Paul" (1661). An expert described the nature of this unique painting in a way that I think illustrates why Paul makes a good retreat director. He wrote:

> Rembrandt's Paul is not a sturdy and forbidding pillar of righteousness but a scruffy, ordinary old man, hapless, weak-chinned and quizzical, gazing at or just past us with arched eyebrows, crumpled brow, a big, fleshy nose and wild tufts of hair escaping from his turban: a humble Paul, on whom God happens to shine the bright consoling light of grace.[4]

Although these words concern a seventeenth-century portrait of Paul—actually Rembrandt's interpretation of the apostle—they may not be that different from some ancient observations about Paul. A late second-century document on Paul and his companions, for instance, describes him thus:

> ...a man small in stature, with a bald head and crooked legs; in a good physical state; with eyebrows that met and a rather hooked nose; full of friendliness, for sometimes he had the appearance of a man and sometimes he had the face of an angel.[5]

This is not an overly flattering portrait, and there is no way to determine how accurate it might be regarding Paul's physical characteristics. It emphasizes, rather, that Paul was a real human person.

We might even surmise from Paul's own letters that his physical presence may have been less than impressive. In 2 Corinthians he acknowledges that some in the community may find him hard to take, "For someone will say, 'His letters are severe and bold, but his bodily presence is weak, and his speech amounts to nothing.'"[6] Moreover, at times his letters indicate that he could be rather short-tempered. He is downright cheeky when he expresses to the Galatians that he wishes that those who are troubling them about reverting to the practice of circumcision would castrate themselves![7] These are forceful words indeed. They might make us think twice about placing ourselves in the hands of such a hotheaded individual.

But this is what makes Paul such a good director. Paul was filled with conviction. He understood that the gospel of Jesus Christ brooks no compromise. He comes across as a real, flesh-and-blood character, someone who experienced life to the full and who struggled on his own with many of the same challenges that all of us face. Paul can be forceful, yes, but he can also be tender and compassionate. He can be obscure and almost incomprehensible at times, but he can also be direct and quite clear about what being a Christian is all about. If we would just give him a chance, I think he can direct us well on this retreat.

Paul's Letters

Before explaining the retreat theme, I must say a word about Paul's letters. They are the primary source of our information on Paul himself and also his teaching and so will be our primary resource for reflection. That means that, if possible, it is helpful to have a Bible at hand. Although I will quote some passages at length, others will only be referenced, owing to the constraints of space. To get the fullest benefit from this retreat, whether individually or as a group, I recommend that you spend time with the biblical passages referred to or quoted. Paul would be the first to affirm that God's Word is the source of true spiritual insight. As with any good retreat director, I think Paul would also admit that the Holy Spirit is truly the director. Paul is merely the vehicle, the window through which we will glimpse the truth that God wishes to impart to us at this time in our lives.

Most importantly, as you work your way through the retreat, you should recognize that Paul can speak directly to you in your life today. Reading his letters is something akin to eavesdropping on an ancient conversation. Unfortunately, we have only one side of that dialogue—Paul's point of view. Missing is the direct viewpoint of his conversation partners— the various individuals or communities he was addressing in his letters. Yet we can get a sense of the profound dialogue that took place between them by reading his letters with openness to their timeless spiritual message. Paul wrote to real people with real problems and questions. His letters were always situation-specific. We are in the same boat. We also have our troubles and our questions. We also seek guidance in our lives. We make a retreat precisely so that we can step back, take a larger view of life, listen more intently for God's Word, and return with a renewed sense of purpose and direction. From this perspective, I believe you will find that Paul will prove to be an excellent spiritual guide.

I also invite you to exercise some imagination during this retreat. Imagination can be a powerful tool in any prayerful experience of meditation. Precisely because Paul is such a real, down-to-earth person, I find it helpful at times to invent imaginative conversations with him about one topic or another based, of course, on his letters. Sometimes during this retreat, I will invite you to allow your imagination to flow freely as we enter into an imaginary conversation with our retreat director or as I recommend reflective exercises. These may cause you to reflect in a more creative fashion.

THE RETREAT THEME

The theme of this retreat is conversion. Although Paul's "road to Damascus" experience is famous, his letters reflect the ongoing nature of conversion—his and our own. We do not find God in a single once-for-all epiphany, but through the hours and countless days of our lives and everyday experiences. We find the treasure of faith in our earthly struggle to live the life to which Jesus calls us. In 2 Corinthians, Paul writes:

> But we have this treasure in clay jars, so that it may be made clear that this extraordinary power belongs to God and does not come from us. We are afflicted in every way, but not crushed; perplexed, but not driven to despair; persecuted, but not forsaken; struck down, but not destroyed; always carrying in the body the death of Jesus, so that the life of Jesus may also be made visible in our bodies. For while we live, we are always being given up to death for Jesus' sake, so that the life of Jesus may be made visible in our mortal flesh.[8]

In this passage Paul is primarily speaking of his experience of ministry. It caused him enormous pain and sacrifice, yet he endured. Indeed, all followers of Jesus have to recognize what Paul understands. Our lives are in reality like fragile earthen vessels. These jars made of clay may evoke the image of small clay lamps used in Paul's day for light or perhaps clay containers used to store sacred writings safely. The vehicles are quite fragile, but the contents are precious.

I think this condition of fragility is true both personally and communally. Individually, each of us knows that we have, as the saying goes, "feet of clay." We know that we have faults that often become stumbling blocks, attitudes or habits that sometimes interfere with good communication and relations. Communally, we know that our society is quite fragile, too. Our world is highly divided into "camps" these days. Everyone protects their own turf. Self-interest, self-promotion and self-advancement are part and parcel of everyday life. For that matter, the tensions caused by possible terrorist activities or crime potential often intervene in our humdrum lives.

There is even fragility in our church. The sexual abuse scandal that erupted in January 2002 and that showed the scandalous failure of some priests, and even some bishops, to protect children rocked the church in the United States to its foundations. As a priest, I found the daily revelations shocking and appalling. Even worse, I was extremely disappointed in the failure of some leaders to act responsibly or to respond to victims in an appropriately pastoral fashion. We learned from this experience that church leaders sometimes fail miserably in their duties and promises. The church has not been crushed by these revelations, but trust has been seriously tarnished.

This experience has exposed the true fragility of the church. We are a communion of saints and sinners.

I submit that whatever our state in life, we have all doubtless faced crisis situations that have taxed our faith and our strength. Our own fragility becomes even more self-evident, and we are confronted again with the perpetual message from God: "Come back to me!" Paul had many such occasions in his life. He acknowledges that it is not easy to follow Jesus and to remain faithful to the gospel. We are all fragile vessels. But the mystery Paul wrestles with is that God chooses fragile, weak vessels and places within them a treasure of infinite value. Finding that treasure requires some serious soul-searching. That is the truth that we must reflect on during this retreat.

OPENING PRAYER

Good and gracious God, giver and sustainer of all life, send me the power of your Holy Spirit to be my guide on this retreat. Open my eyes and ears to the message of your servant, Paul the Apostle, so that I might hear and understand the profound truth that he imparts. Give me the strength to persevere every day in my faith, so that I will not become discouraged when life's troubles keep pounding on my door. Give me courage to embrace whatever comes my way and to recognize that you do not place on my own fragile shoulders any task that I cannot bear. For your grace alone sustains me in faith, and I place all that I am once more and always in your loving care. I pray this through your Son Jesus and the Holy Spirit, now and forever. Amen.

RETREAT SESSION ONE
Scriptures for Reflection

> From now on, therefore, we regard no one from a human point of view; even though we once knew Christ from a human point of view, we know him no longer in that way. So if anyone is in Christ, there is a new creation: everything old has passed away; see, everything has become new! (2 Corinthians 5:16–17)

> For neither circumcision nor uncircumcision is anything; but a new creation is everything! (Galatians 6:15)

Finding a starting point for Paul's spirituality is tricky. Exactly where is the entry point into Paul's understanding of how the coming of Jesus Christ has changed the world? The passage above from 2 Corinthians is a good starting point.

Anyone who has read all of Paul's letters will recognize that one of his most profound yet simple thoughts in them is expressed by two words: "in Christ." From Paul's perspective, being "in Christ" is what the spiritual life is all about. Whatever happened to him on the road to Damascus, the end result was a tremendous transformation of Paul's life. If it should not be characterized as a conversion in the sense of a change in religions, it is nevertheless a conversion in the sense of a dramatic turnabout. He who was headed to Damascus to persecute followers of Jesus suddenly was knocked to the ground and directed to "Straight Street."[9] God issued Paul a direct invitation to straighten out his life. He was headed in the wrong direction. He was on a "crooked" path. As Flannery O'Connor, the great Catholic short-story writer, humorously remarked: "I reckon the Lord knew the only way to make a Christian out of that one was to knock him off his horse!"[10]

For Paul this was merely the beginning of a complete transformation. A personal encounter with the risen Lord Jesus dramatically means reorienting one's entire perspective. The human way of perception gives way to the divine perspective. For those who are truly "in Christ"[11]—incorporated into the "body of Christ" by baptism and transformed by grace—everything seems new. Paul's phrase is distinctive. Being "in Christ" makes one an entirely new creation! It's like a fresh start. The allusion refers to God's own act of creation at the beginning.[12] God spoke and the universe sprang into being. For Paul, Christ spoke to him by means of a mysterious revelation, thereby creating him anew. In both instances of creation, God is clearly the principal actor and the cause of the effect. Conversions don't happen under our own power. God provides the grace, the spiritual fuel, if you will, to be transformed.

Paul acknowledges that he experienced a revelation, a supernatural unveiling of God's will. He received an appearance of the risen Jesus that empowered this transformation in his life. The good news for us is that we, too, can experience this same transformation. Paul's call was not exclusive. Paul's experience is proof that one does not have to have literally lived with Jesus of Nazareth and walked with him and witnessed his teaching and miracles in order to be called by him. Paul became an apostle, sent on a mission, by the call of the risen Lord. Paul came to know him as Lord, Savior and Redeemer.

In fact, "Lord" is Paul's most important title for Jesus in his risen state. In the Old Testament, "Lord" was a title reserved for God. Paul's application of the title to Jesus was tantamount to calling him God, acknowledging his divine status. This was a dramatic move that the early Christians made, and it is still the basis of our faith. Jesus is Lord, and he continues to call others, like ourselves, across time to continue the mission of proclaiming the gospel message. Like Paul, we can receive a call from the Lord.

On retreat what grace can I seek that would truly transform my life? Unlike Paul perhaps, most conversions are slow processes that take place over time.[13] That is not to deny quick conversions but to recognize that they are rare. Paul did not expect his communities to have the very same experience that he had on the road to Damascus. He did, however, expect them to surrender to God's grace and to submit to the transformation that comes with life in Christ. He urged them to become new creations in the Lord Jesus.

In his Letter to the Galatians, Paul uses the same expression, "new creation," in a different context: "For neither circumcision nor uncircumcision is anything; but a new creation is everything."[14] He had been upset at the Galatians because they were deserting the gospel message he had given them and were reverting to former practices acquired as Jews, in particular, male circumcision. He forcefully states that life in Christ changes all that. The issue is not whether one is circumcised (to reinforce Jewish identity) or not (to assert gentile identity). Christ has changed this reality. As Paul wrote to the Galatians: "There is no longer Jew or Greek, there is no longer slave or free, there is no longer male and female; for all of you are one in Christ Jesus."[15] Nothing else matters than to surrender to Christ. He urges the Galatians to become a new creation and to leave behind their past identity. Christ makes all things new. Being "in Christ" makes us new.

So profound was this transformation for Paul that he even says to the Philippians that he no longer considered his former life as a Pharisee to count for anything, in comparison to what he gained in Christ.

> Yet whatever gains I had, these I have come to regard as loss because of Christ. More than that, I regard everything as loss because of the surpassing value of knowing Christ Jesus my Lord. For his sake I have suffered the loss of all things, and I regard them as rubbish, in order that I may gain Christific....[16]

Are you prepared for such a profound transformation? It could just happen on this retreat.

Consider this retreat God's personal invitation to you. God seeks to be closer to you than you can imagine. God is also aware that your life is most likely like everyone else's—a bit of a jumble and not always headed in the right direction. We know just how fragile our lives can be. And perhaps we say from time to time as we see others' lives crumble, "There, but for the grace of God, go I." We need to heed God's invitation to conversion. As a billboard in the South expressed it: "God loves you just the way you are, but He loves you too much to leave you that way." The invitation will require leaving something behind and going to something quite new. But, as Paul experienced it, it is well worth the effort.

In my personal experience, I have had periodic conversions. These have usually been slow "turnings" and gradual awakenings. For me, life in Christ has been a bit of the dance of life, halting steps here and there, forward and backward, but always moving. Once when I was on a college retreat, I had an overwhelming sense of my sinfulness and unworthiness in

God's eyes. It took place during a reconciliation service. I can't explain what really happened, though it occurred during a period in which I was discerning whether to become a priest or not. After the examination of conscience, I suddenly found myself crying. Now, as my friends would testify, I am not given to emotional displays, so this was highly unusual. What was worse, I couldn't stop it. I am sure the people around me were looking at me with curiosity, wondering, "What's his problem?!"

Later, during a spiritual direction conference, I realized that I had indeed been touched by God's grace during that retreat. From that time on, I saw reality differently. I felt much closer to Jesus Christ than ever before. It was as if Jesus now walked with me on the journey of life. I continued to struggle with my vocation as a priest (though you obviously know that I made it), but my sense of the love of Christ for me and for those whom I felt called to serve was incredibly powerful. My own conversion is surely ongoing, but I believe I have glimpsed quite concretely what Paul meant when he spoke of his transformed life in Christ. Elsewhere he suggests just how profound this transformation is: "it is no longer I who live, but it is Christ who lives in me."[17]

Now that is a profound change: To be so transformed that we no longer live in ourselves but allow Christ to live in us, so that all we do and all we are reflects Christ to the world. This is a worthy goal for any retreat, to be so transformed. With the aid of our brother, Paul the Apostle, let us pray for the courage to accept this invitation to become a new creation in Christ.

FOR REFLECTION

Describe your own life "in Christ." How would you characterize your relationship with Jesus Christ?

As you reflect upon your personal journey of faith, can you discern distinctive moments of "conversion," times when you have truly been "turned around" by God's grace? Have there been moments of dramatic change? Times of more gradual transformation?

In what ways have you become a "new creation" through your faith?

Quietly read over the passage from 2 Corinthians 4:7–11 quoted above. What are the fragile areas of your own life? How do you respond to them? What is the "treasure" within your own fragile existence?

CLOSING PRAYER

Lord Jesus, you revealed yourself long ago to your servant Paul. You invited him to enter into the mystery of new life in you. Hide not your resurrected face from me. Transform my fragile existence into a new creation. Help me find the treasure you have placed deep within me that I might be comforted by your love. Come and make known to me your will that I may surrender myself completely to it. Transform me by your grace, Lord, that I may more worthily lead the life to which you call me. Amen.

Notes

1. 2 Peter 3:15b–17.
2. "Homilies on the Epistle to the Romans," in *Nicene and Post-Nicene Fathers*, vol. 11, p. 335, excerpted from *The AGES Digital Library Collections*, Version 2.0 (Albany, Ore.: AGES Software, 1997).
3. See "Joint Declaration on the Doctrine of Justification," *Origins* 28:8 (July 16, 1998), pp. 120–127. On July 23, 2006, the World Methodist Conference signed onto this joint declaration while meeting in Seoul, South Korea. Thus, three major denominations have now expressed a common understanding of Paul's notion of justification, a significant ecumenical advance.
4. Michael Kimmelman, "Humanity with Flaws Forgiven," *The New York Times* (January 28, 2005), p. B39. Kimmelman's comment builds upon those made by Arthur K. Wheelock, Jr., the curator of the exhibit.
5. From "The Acts of Paul and Thecla," 2 (author's translation). One can find an English translation of the full text in Wilhelm Schneemelcher and Edgar Hennecke, eds., *New Testament Apocrypha* (Louisville, Ky.: Westminster/John Knox, 1992), vol. 2, pp. 239–246.
6. 2 Corinthians 10:10, author's translation.
7. See Galatians 5:12.
8. 2 Corinthians 4:7–11.
9. See Acts 9:11.
10. Flannery O'Connor, *The Habit of Being*, Sally Fitzgerald, ed. (New York: Farrar, Straus, Giroux, 1979), pp. 354–355.
11. Paul also uses the similar expressions "in Christ Jesus" (Romans 8:1; 16:3) and "in the Lord" (1 Thessalonians 3:8; Romans 16:22). They are synonymous. Interestingly, Paul has a preference for placing the word "Christ" (from Greek *christos* meaning "messiah; anointed one") before the name "Jesus." Elsewhere the New Testament speaks more often of Jesus Christ, i.e., Jesus Messiah. Paul's distinctive usage helped to make "Christ" as much a name as a title.
12. See Genesis 1:1–2:3.
13. For a fuller explanation of the biblical understanding of conversion, see Ronald D. Witherup, *Conversion in the New Testament*, Zacchaeus New Testament Studies (Collegeville, Minn.: Liturgical, 1994).

14. Galatians 6:15.
15. Galatians 3:28. See also Romans 10:12; 1 Corinthians 12:13; Colossians 3:11.
16. Philippians 3:7–8.
17. Galatians 2:20.

DAY TWO

BEING CALLED, JUSTIFIED AND SAVED BY GRACE

COMING TOGETHER IN THE SPIRIT

O LORD, you have searched me and known me.
You know when I sit down and when I rise up;
   you discern my thoughts from far away.
You search out my path and my lying down,
   and are acquainted with all my ways.
Even before a word is on my tongue,
   O LORD, you know it completely.
You hem me in, behind and before,
   and lay your hand upon me.
Such knowledge is too wonderful for me;
   it is so high that I cannot attain it.

Where can I go from your spirit?
   Or where can I flee from your presence?
If I ascend to heaven, you are there;
   if I make my bed in Sheol, you are there.

If I take the wings of the morning
   and settle at the farthest limits of the sea,
even there your hand shall lead me,
   and your right hand shall hold me fast.
If I say, "Surely the darkness shall cover me,
   and the light around me become night,"
even the darkness is not dark to you;
   the night is as bright as the day,
   for darkness is as light to you.

For it was you who formed my inward parts;
   you knit me together in my mother's womb.
I praise you, for I am fearfully and wonderfully made.
   Wonderful are your works;
that I know very well.
—Psalm 139:1–14

In writing Psalm 139, the psalmist has expressed a profound truth: God has called each of us into existence from our very conception, and God knows us better than we know ourselves. There is no escaping God. No matter where we think we can flee, God is there, tracking us down, not to bother us but to bestow love upon us. God is like the "hound of heaven" from Francis Thompson's famous poem of the same title:

I fled Him, down the nights and down the days;
I fled Him, down the arches of the years;
I fled Him, down the labyrinthine ways
Of my own mind; in the mist of tears
I hid from Him, and under running laughter.
Up vistaed hopes I sped;
And shot, precipitated,

Adown Titanic glooms of chasmèd fears,
From those strong Feet that followed, followed after.
But with unhurrying chase,
And unperturbèd pace,
...
(For, though I knew His love Who followèd,
Yet was I sore adread
Lest, having Him, I must have naught beside.)...[1]

The poem, as well as the psalm, recalls that God never ceases to reach out in love. God hounds us for reasons of love. God follows us and is closer than we can ever know because God is the one who bestowed our identity upon us. Life is all about being called, justified and saved by grace—that is what Paul would have us know.

In this retreat session we will concentrate on Paul's understanding of the identity God bestows on each one of us. Paul was conscious that the risen Jesus had called him by name and sent him on a special mission. It began a series of interrelated events that changed Paul's life forever. He also came to understand that God had freely bestowed righteousness, living uprightly before God and human beings, upon him. God's grace had saved him. All he had to do was respond to that grace willingly. The same can be said for each of us.

OPENING PRAYER

God of all life, from of old you have gathered a people to yourself so that all might reflect your glory in creation. As with the ancient prophets, you have called me by name and marked me forever with the sign of your love. I stand in awe of this grace. I ask now that you keep me always in the palm of your hand.

Never let me stray from that love. Make me always thankful of your gift of life, and continue to mold me into the likeness of your beloved Son, Jesus, my Lord and Savior, who reigns with you and the Holy Spirit now and forever. Amen.

Retreat Session Two
Scriptures for Reflection

We know that all things work together for good for those who love God, who are called according to his purpose. For those whom he foreknew he also predestined to be conformed to the image of his Son, in order that he might be the firstborn among many sisters and brothers. And those whom he predestined he also called; and those whom he called he also justified; and those whom he justified he also glorified. (Romans 8:28–30; author's translation)

Do not fear, for I have redeemed you; I have called you by name, you are mine. (Isaiah 43:1)

To say that Paul had a lot of self-confidence is probably an understatement. I pointed out in the introduction that Paul's personality is partly what makes him such an interesting retreat director. I suspect some would have considered him quite arrogant, though. He felt no compunction in telling people his own view of things. He was even so bold as to confront the "pillars" of the church, like Peter and James the brother of the Lord.[2] But if we view such actions as evidence of arrogance, then we seriously miss the point. Paul's confidence is not arrogance; rather, it stems from his faith in God.

If we pick apart the passage from Romans quoted above in the Scripture reflection, we find that Paul confidently asserts four major points:

1) God has a plan or purpose for the universe.
2) This plan encompasses a series of actions upon human beings that follow a pre-established pattern of foreknowledge, predestination, calling, justifying and glorifying.
3) God's purpose is to shape everyone in the model of his Son (Jesus Christ) in order to produce one grand family, all brothers and sisters in the Lord.
4) For those who love God, everything will ultimately work out for the good.

This is certainly a sweeping vision. It shows that Paul believes he is privy to God's plan. We are destined for glory. We have been predestined, not in the sense that we have no choice in the matter, but in the sense that God desires our ultimate good and has created us for this purpose. We are called and justified, that is, placed in an upright relationship with God by God's own grace. And we are bound for glory because that is where Jesus has gone, and he has preceded us as the "first fruits" of this glory by means of his resurrection.[3]

What gives Paul confidence that he has penetrated this mysterious realm of God's plan?

I think we should look to Paul's experience on the road to Damascus as a likely source of this confidence. The book of Acts gives us the only narrative account of this event (three times, no less!).[4] You know the story well. Paul is on a journey to Damascus to arrest followers of Jesus Christ and bring them back to Jerusalem in chains. While underway, he suddenly falls to the ground in a blinding light and hears a voice that cries out, "Saul, Saul, why do you persecute me?"[5] In response to Paul's question about who is confronting him, the voice says, "I am Jesus, whom you are persecuting."[6] Paul is then

given directions to proceed to Damascus, blinded and help-
less, where it is revealed that he will become the apostle to the
gentiles. His life thus took what we might call a spiritual
U-turn. The chief persecutor paradoxically became the chief
proponent of the new faith.

Paul's letters do not describe this conversion experience—
really more of a divine call—in such detail. Rather, as pointed
out in the introduction, Paul calls his experience a "revelation," a miraculous unveiling of the identity of Jesus Christ by
means of God's grace.[7] By revelation Paul came to know his
Lord and Savior. While Paul does not get specific as to how he
saw and understood this revelation, we can say with assurance
that it was a life-transforming experience that opened an
entirely new vista for Paul. He had never dreamed that God
could touch his heart so deeply, so movingly, that he would be
a changed man forever. But what did this mean for Paul?

Let's call upon our imagination to further our reflection.
What if we unexpectedly had the chance to interview Paul and
get him to flesh out his experience? Here is how I think such a
conversation might go....

RW: Pardon me, Saint Paul, for disturbing you. I hope you
don't mind, but I would like to ask you a few questions about
your writings that have intrigued me.

Paul: You don't have to be so formal. We are all "saints"—
the elect called by God. You can call me by my given name,
Saul, though I gather you are a gentile. Just call me Paul.

RW: OK, if you insist. Let me get right to the point. I have
always been fascinated with how strong and secure a vision
you have for the salvation of the world. You have such confidence that things will work out for good because that's God's

plan. Can you tell me how you came to that understanding?

Paul: Well, first let me remind you that I probably always came across as rather secure in my positions. Even as a child, I suppose my parents thought of me as basically stubborn. When I was a young man, filled with boundless energy and vigor, I was really attracted to the Pharisees. After all, they were such a zealous group. To my mind, they represented all that is good in Judaism, trying to preserve our heritage and our identity. I admit I directed all my energy into the Pharisaic party. I always admired the Pharisees and their enthusiasm for our faith. And I never denied that I went so far as to persecute the church. I suppose it was just a natural result of my strong convictions. But God had other thoughts. God was the one who decided to redirect my energies. He reached out and touched me. By revealing his Son Christ Jesus to me, I saw reality in a whole new way. And I never turned back.

RW: The story of your conversion and call has always fascinated me. I wonder, can you tell me what it was really like? Your colleague Luke describes it in great detail but you don't seem to do that in your letters.

Paul: Ah, my friend Luke. He had a way with words. He was a good writer and a loyal companion. But for me, the details of my call were not the most important thing. Oh, I remembered that day very clearly. How could I forget? Falling to the ground...the blinding light. I felt that Jesus had hunted me down. The strong voice that called me by name and asked me that haunting question: "Why do you persecute me?" But honestly, it all happened so fast, and I became so disoriented. I remember getting up. I panicked. I couldn't see a thing. I felt like a baby. I had to be led by the hand into Damascus. I was introduced to people I had never heard of, and to tell the truth, I was as frightened of them as they were of me. But I digress.

How does one really put into words what I felt that day and many days thereafter? Christ Jesus had spoken to *me*. I could scarcely believe it. He had called *me*. The Lord of the universe had appeared to *me*. I never imagined I could have deserved his attention. After all, I was doing everything in my power to destroy those who believed in his name.

It's his voice I remember most. It was as if I was the only one in the world. He spoke to me in such a way that, well, all I can say is that I felt his presence in the depths of my being. It was as if I no longer knew myself. He knew me better. And he trusted me. I can never forget that. He trusted me with a mission. And I saw that what he represented was real truth, real light, real love. And I trusted him. If I had to be led by the hand, so be it. I knew he would not let me down. I could practically feel his love burning a hole in my soul. It was such a cleansing experience.

RW: But how did you realize the importance of this event for your life?

Paul: Well, it took me some time to really understand what had happened to me. Naturally, after I was baptized, I got acquainted with some others who believed in Jesus as the Christ. I got to talking with them, and I learned a few things about Jesus, of course. And I heard a lot about the "pillars of the church," you know, Cephas (Peter), John, James the brother of the Lord and others. But you should know I did not rely on their approval. I didn't need it. Jesus himself had called me to be the apostle to the gentiles, and that is what I set about doing right away. I just understood that if Jesus had called me, then I should respond. And that is what I did. It was all grace. I couldn't believe how my life had changed. And I can assure you that this turn of events startled my family and friends.

RW: You use the language of "new creation" in your letters. Is that what you mean by this change?

Paul: Well, I am glad that you picked up on that phrase. Yes, it is that different. You see, before I knew Jesus Christ personally, I thought I had to do something concrete to earn God's approval. That's why I was so zealous about keeping the law. I just didn't see that it was the other way around. God already had granted me approval. He had formed me in the womb. He knew me inside and out. He had already called me into existence. And by God's grace, I had already been made upright in God's eyes. That's why I called it "justified." God has set me right. Of course, he practically needed to knock me senseless to do it. It wasn't anything I did; it was what God's grace did in me. God really changed me. In Christ Jesus, I became a new man, a new creation. I was truly saved. And nothing else mattered after that.

RW: You speak often about salvation and being saved. I wonder if you could explain it in a little more detail.

Paul: I am surprised you even need to ask me that. Isn't it obvious what salvation is? The human condition is so fleeting, so finite, so corruptible, and the world is in such need of transformation, that salvation is the only remedy. Only God can save. God saves us from sin, from death, from the corruptibility of the world. And most importantly, in Jesus, God saves us from ourselves. We are our own worst enemies. We don't even realize sometimes how much in need of being saved we are. I suppose we just get too immersed in our everyday activities.

But, son, I am telling you, salvation is everything. By his cross and resurrection, Jesus Christ has saved us and has set us on the path to glory. He's the one who truly sanctifies us. He went before us, by his cross and resurrection, as the first fruits of the new creation. When he finally comes in judgment and in vindication, then you will really know salvation in all its effects. But mark my words, you've already been justified and saved. You just need to live more like it.

And now, if you don't mind, I have to get going. I have to get to a wrestling match. And let me be quite frank—I think you should dwell a little bit more on what I wrote in my letters. You might have fewer questions!

RW: Thank you, Paul, for taking the time to explain a bit more. I promise I will go back to your letters. But if I may be so bold to say, I never seem to read them without coming up with more questions than answers.

And so might such an imaginary conversation go.... I suspect if we actually could converse with Paul, he would be surprised at some of our questions and observations. He wrote in a much different period of history, and some of his language is simply hard to get a handle on. But we can be certain of this: Paul wrote with conviction. He strongly believed that his basic message—the gospel or good news—was that Jesus Christ's death on the cross and his resurrection had significantly changed reality. In Christ, all became a new creation. Salvation had come definitively in an entirely new form.

Paul's confidence in God's salvation was not a naïve hope. On the contrary, Paul recognized that sin was still a problem, in the world and in his own life. But he had a remarkable insight into the boundless generosity of God. He reminded the Romans of it when he wrote:

> For while we were still weak, at the right time Christ died for the ungodly. Indeed, rarely will anyone die for a righteous person—though perhaps for a good person someone might actually dare to die. *But God proves his love for us in that while we still were sinners Christ died for us.*[8]

The highlighted words contain an incredibly comforting assertion. "While we were still sinners" God acted on our behalf. God did not wait for us to change our lives, to reform our sinfulness or to "get our act together" before sending his own Son. Instead, God sent Jesus while we remained in our sinful state.

We should not underestimate the importance of Paul's perspective on sin and salvation. I have known many people who, when confronted with the question of putting their faith in action, or starting to attend church, or getting interested in a community of faith, have tried to dodge the issue on the pretense that they are not worthy. The tendency is to delay the decision of faith. Some may think, "I am not ready for this. I don't think I could fit into a group of believers. I still need to reform my life. I'll get around to it once I have set everything in order."

There is no time like the present. God does not wait for you to change your life before he comes knocking on your door. God did not wait for either the Jews or the gentiles in the first century to get things right. God did not finally send his Son, a Savior, after humanity had gotten the message right. Instead, God sent his Son just at the right time, just when we needed salvation the most. Perhaps we should recall Jesus' own words:

"Those who are well have no need of a physician, but those who are sick; I have come to call not the righteous but sinners."[9] In fact, Jesus scandalized people in his day precisely because he reached out to sinners. But that is why he came: to heal what needed to be healed and to forgive what needed to be forgiven. This is really what Paul reminds us of by his own message. He understood that, in Christ, God had acted toward all humanity in the most gracious manner imaginable. And these words can remind us of our call as we enter into this retreat. God is reaching out to us now, wherever we are in our lives at present.

In short, Paul understood that God had called him, justified him and saved him by grace. He drew comfort from the fact that God acted on his behalf and on behalf of all humanity even while we continue struggling to live upright lives, worthy of the divine identity that has been bestowed on us.

To draw this session to a close, I am reminded of the familiar Christian hymn, "Amazing Grace."[10] Its comforting words hark back to some of Paul's insights. They provide a poetic way to draw our reflections together.

> Amazing Grace, how sweet the sound,
> That saved a wretch like me
> I once was lost, but now am found,
> Was blind, but now I see.

> 'Twas Grace that taught my heart to fear,
> And Grace my fears relieved;
> How precious did that Grace appear
> The hour I first believed!

> Through many dangers, toils, and snares,

I have already come;
'Tis grace has brought me safe thus far,
And grace will lead me home.

The Lord has promised good to me,
His word my hope secures!
He will my shield and portion be,
As long as life endures.

...

When we've been there ten thousand years,
Bright shining as the sun,
We've no less days to sing God's praise
Than when we'd first begun.

FOR REFLECTION

Read Romans 8:28–39. In this passage Paul expresses his irrepressible confidence that despite all kinds of obstacles, nothing can separate us from God's love. Can you compose (mentally or in writing) a similar list of obstacles that seem to interfere with your hopefulness in life? Do you have the same confidence as Paul that everything will eventually work out for good?

Make a list of your good qualities and a list of your faults. Does the one outweigh the other? What do you think Paul would do with such a list? How would he bring it to prayer before God and how would he surrender himself to God's will? Can you imitate Paul in this exercise?

Slowly read Psalm 139:1–14, which began this session. It is a poetic reflection on the mystery of every individual human life. When you pray these words, can you imagine God's grace pumping through your veins? God has called you by name and bestowed a gracious identity upon you. God is closer to you than you can imagine. Thank God in your own words for the gift of this identity.

Sit reflectively for a time with Francis Thompson's poetic image of "the hound of heaven." God is pursuing you out of love. How do you see God reaching out to you in your life? How do you feel about the notion that God consistently seeks you out? What kind of response do you think God is asking of you?

Closing Prayer

(Make the following prayer from Paul's Letter to the Romans your own as you give thanks for the great gift of salvation that God has bestowed on us all.)

O the depth of the riches and wisdom and knowledge of God! How unsearchable are his judgments and how inscrutable his ways! "For who has known the mind of the Lord? Or who has been his counselor?" "Or who has given a gift to him, to receive a gift in return?" For from him and through him and to him are all things. To him be the glory forever. Amen. (Romans 11:33–36)

Notes

1. Francis Thompson, "The Hound of Heaven," in *A Pocket Book of Modern Verse*, Oscar Williams, ed. (New York: Washington Square, 1954), p. 112.
2. See Galatians 2:2, 9.
3. See 1 Corinthians 15:20, 23.
4. See Acts 9:1–9; 22:1–21; 26:12–18.
5. Acts 9:4.
6. Acts 9:5.
7. Galatians 1:15–16.

8. Romans 5:6–8, emphasis added.
9. Mark 2:17; see also Matthew 9:12 and Luke 5:31.
10. The first four verses go back to John Newton (1725–1807); the fifth verse is attributed to John Rees (c. 1859). The origin of the tune is unknown, but it may have originated among African–American slaves.

DAY THREE

EMBRACING
THE
CROSS
OF
JESUS
CHRIST

COMING TOGETHER IN THE SPIRIT

In his bestselling book *Tuesdays with Morrie*, Mitch Albom describes an encounter with his favorite former professor, Morrie, who is dying of Lou Gehrig's disease. It offers a poignant perspective on suffering.

> "Okay, question," I say to Morrie. His bony fingers hold his glasses across his chest, which rises and falls with each labored breath.
> "What's the question?" he says.
> "Remember the book of Job?"
> "From the Bible?"
> "Right. Job is a good man, but God makes him suffer. To test his faith."
> "I remember."
> "Takes away everything he has, his house, his money, his family."
> "His health."
> "Makes him sick."

"To test his faith."

"Right. To test his faith. So I'm wondering."

"What are you wondering?"

"What do you think about that?"

Morrie coughs violently, his hands quiver as he drops them to his side.

"I think," he says, smiling, "God overdid it." [1]

The mystery of suffering, especially by innocent people, is a perennial problem. It has caused philosophers and writers of all stripes to pen profound treatises in an effort to make sense of the mystery. No doubt any one of us may have felt exactly like Morrie at one time or another: God has really overdone it in my case. Or maybe we have felt like Job, the quintessential sufferer in the Bible, whose multiple misfortunes caused him to curse the day he was born. [2] Although the book of Job is likely the best-known biblical book on the topic, Paul is no slouch in his own reflections. In fact, he has many profound thoughts on suffering. On this day of our retreat, we are going to focus on Paul's approach to this topic and why he believes that suffering—symbolized by the cross—is an essential part of living the Christian message.

OPENING PRAYER

(To Christ crucified; while holding or gazing upon a crucifix or a picture of the crucifixion)

O loving Savior, when I gaze upon you hanging on the cross of our salvation, I am brought low by my own weakness to endure even the least bit of suffering that comes my way. I look to you for strength, to you who were able not only to endure the most humiliating and painful of deaths, but also to forgive those who committed this injustice against you. Make me strong, Lord, when I am tempted to flee in the face of pain and rejection. And give me patience with and the ability to forgive those who cause me pain. Let me say with your servant Paul, "I have been crucified with Christ," so that I might indeed share the resurrection. Amen.

RETREAT SESSION THREE
Scriptures for Reflection
> For Jews demand signs and Greeks desire wisdom, but we proclaim Christ crucified, a stumbling block to Jews and foolishness to Gentiles, but to those who are the called, both Jews and Greeks, Christ the power of God and the wisdom of God. (1 Corinthians 1:22–24)

> For I decided to know nothing among you except Jesus Christ, and him crucified. And I came to you in weakness and in fear and in much trembling. My speech and my proclamation were not with plausible words of wisdom, but with a demonstration of the Spirit and of power, so that your faith might rest not on human wisdom but on the power of God. (1 Corinthians 2:2–5)

As I pointed out in the introduction to this book, Paul lived in a complex, multicultural and multilingual world. Two of the most far-reaching influences on his life were Judaism and the Greco-Roman (Hellenistic) world in which he lived and worked. At the very outset of his first letter to his beloved Corinthians, Paul acknowledges these two distinctive worldviews. In essence, he admits that the content of his gospel message—Christ crucified—fits into neither worldview. The Jews find it a stumbling block (*skandalon* in Greek, from which we derive our English word *scandal*). They would prefer to have a more powerful sign of God's presence. The Greeks find it foolishness (*morian* in Greek, related to our English words *moron* and *moronic*). They would prefer to have a sound philosophical presentation to convince them intellectually of what to do. In other words, a crucified Christ makes no sense in terms of any worldly evaluation. Yet Paul insists that both Jew and Greek alike are called to follow Christ. The cross is central to being a Christian. It is a paradoxical sign that communicates victory over loss, weakness transformed into strength and triumph over tragedy. It is the crucified Christ alone who is true power and wisdom.

Suffering, we know, is part of the human condition. Some of it is actually caused by the terrible acts of violent individuals bent on reaping destruction in the name of whatever cause. The terrible tragedy of terrorism, such as the September 11, 2001, attacks on the United States or the suicide bombers in the Middle East and elsewhere, are examples. Some suffering comes in the form of tremendous natural disasters, such as the devastating hurricanes in Florida and the Gulf Coast in 2005 and the overwhelming Asian tsunami in late 2004. Yet other forms of suffering accompany the human condition: incurable diseases, the results of accidents, psychological and emotional stress, broken and strained relationships or simply the pressures of daily life. All suffering, however, presents a challenge to all humanity. And innocent suffering is an even more vexing question. What do we make of this suffering, and how do we react to it?

Paul was no stranger to suffering. Indeed, he seems to draw attention to suffering as an inherent part of what it means to follow Christ and what it means to be an apostle. In particular, Paul is aware that proclaiming the truth can lead to much suffering and rejection. At various points in his letters he lists the number of serious challenges he had to undergo for the sake of the gospel message. Second Corinthians provides an eloquent defense of his apostleship by drawing attention to an incredible list of hardships he endured.

> Are they ministers of Christ? (I am talking foolishly)—I am a better one: with far greater labors, far more imprisonments, with countless floggings, and often near death. Five times I received from the Jews the forty lashes minus one. Three times I was beaten with rods. Once I was stoned. Three times I was shipwrecked; for a night and a day I was adrift at sea; on frequent journeys, in danger from rivers, danger from bandits, danger from my own people, danger from Gentiles, danger in the city, danger in the wilderness, danger at sea, danger from false brothers; in toil and hardship, through many a sleepless night, hungry and thirsty, often without food, cold and naked. And, besides other things, there is the daily pressure of my anxiety for all the churches. Who is weak, and I am not weak? Who is made to stumble, and I am not indignant? If I must boast, I will boast of the things that show my weakness. The God and Father of the Lord Jesus (blessed be he forever!) knows that I do not lie. In Damascus, the governor under King Aretas guarded the city of Damascus in order to seize me, but I was let down in a basket through the wall, and escaped from his hands.[3]

What a catalogue of misadventures! How much could one person endure? This list of trials and tribulations is worthy of any Hollywood movie of the proverbial hero or heroine who willingly endures every kind of challenge imaginable, trudges on in life, and comes out victorious. But that is not Paul's purpose.

What we should not miss in such a seemingly boastful catalogue of sufferings is that Paul sees a profound paradox at work in his life. In the world's eyes, anyone who would endure what Paul claims would be seen as foolish, weak and ineffective. He would rightly be the object of ridicule. But this is exactly what Paul turns on its head. He says it well later in the same letter:

> Therefore I am content with weaknesses, insults, hardships, persecutions, and calamities for the sake of Christ; for whenever I am weak, then I am strong.[4]

That is the Christian paradox, according to Paul. What in worldly terms is perceived as weakness is actually strength. No symbol so embodies this truth as the cross. Life in Christ means embracing the cross. It requires not that we flee from suffering but that we accept it and learn to live with it constructively. Paul even seems to flaunt his sufferings as an apostle as a kind of badge of honor. They confirm that he has testified to the truth of the gospel message.

One cannot help but wonder, however, how realistic Paul's vision is. Isn't it overly idealistic to think that most of us human beings can not only endure suffering gracefully but also embrace it? In other words, is Paul serious when he speaks of the need to see in the cross the paradox of power in weakness? Would he not scream out like the suffering prophet Jeremiah, "Cursed be the day on which I was born! / The day when my mother bore me, let it not be blessed!"?[5] Paul doubtless had bleak days in the midst of his trials and tribulations. Would he not bemoan his fate like Job, who at the beginning of his terrible calamities cries out, "Why did I not die at birth, come forth from the womb and expire?"[6] Didn't Paul ever have one of those proverbial "days from hell" in which everything goes wrong and the whole world seems like a grand conspiracy to wreak havoc in one's life? Was Paul never tempted to give up—to throw in the towel, as we say—in the face of the incredible hurdles that he encountered in his missionary endeavors?

Frankly, few of us are truly stoical when confronted with such adversity. But, in fact, Paul is not only sincere in his convictions but also has a good foundation for them. Jesus himself is the reason for Paul's confidence. Jesus should also be the reason for our confidence.

For Paul, the Christian faith was born in suffering. Jesus willingly took on the humiliating and excruciating torture of death by crucifixion so that he could show others the way to victory through suffering. Jesus is the model who gives confidence to Paul. When he urges his communities to imitate him as he imitates Christ, he is neither arrogant nor naïve.[7] Rather, he is invoking the profound meaning of faith. Paul expressed this faith well when he took over an early Christian hymn, slightly modified it, and made it a model to emulate.

> *Let the same mind be in you that was in Christ Jesus,*
> > *who, though he was in the form of God,*
> > > *did not regard equality with God*
> > > *as something to be exploited,*
> > *but emptied himself,*

taking the form of a slave,
being born in human likeness.
And being found in human form,
he humbled himself
and became obedient to the point of death—
even death on a cross.
Therefore God also highly exalted him
and gave him the name
that is above every name,
so that at the name of Jesus
every knee should bend,
in heaven and on earth and under the earth,
and every tongue should confess
that Jesus Christ is Lord,
to the glory of God the Father.[8]

One can discern two parts to this magnificent passage. The first part is all about Christ Jesus humbling himself in three ways. First, he freely set aside his divine status, that is, emptied himself of his Godhead. Second, he took on human form, the form of a "slave." Finally, he accepted death, even the humiliating and excruciating death of crucifixion.

An intriguing aspect of Paul's understanding is that, using the model of Jesus, he makes a virtue of becoming a slave—not literally, but metaphorically. Like Jesus, we become slaves (or servants) for the sake of others, slaves of righteousness. Paradoxically, it frees us to live in a carefree manner. This means that we do not worry about whether our lives conform to every jot and tittle of God's law. Rather, our entire life is oriented toward service for others. Everything we do as a "slave of Christ" contributes toward building up the community, not tearing it down. Becoming a "slave of Christ" prepares us to undergo suffering for the sake of the truth, for the sake of the gospel and for the sake of others.[9] It is a truly humbling experience.

The second part of the passage is the exaltation that paradoxically has come about because of this voluntary act of suffering, in obedience to his Father's will. The hymn noticeably has a turning point that illustrates Paul's message clearly. The "therefore" in verse 9 indicates that the suffering Christ endured was the reason for his exaltation.[10] Suffering, the utter experience of weakness and vulnerability, became the means for his vindication by his heavenly Father. Obedience to his Father's will, even to the point of the ignominious death on the cross, results in God's exaltation of his Son. God rewards weakness borne with the strength of faith, perseverance and endurance. Our vindication is not necessarily visible or immediate. But it is, says Paul, inevitable for those with faith.

Perhaps an even more remarkable perspective on the cross is found in Galatians. Paul boldly says:

> May I never boast of anything except the cross of our Lord Jesus Christ, by which the world has been crucified to me, and I to the world.[11]

Paul expresses here the understanding that he participates in Christ's crucifixion, which is the essential symbol of what it means to follow Christ, by the marks he bears in his ministry. He is bound to the world not by means of human values, but by new Christian values, in which the cross means everything. In the context of the passage, Paul contrasts the ones among the Galatians who are agitating the community and boasting that they bear the "marks" of identity that God insists on, namely, circumcision. Paul retorts that he bears even more authentic "marks," those of crucifixion. He will boast in nothing but the cross of Christ. It has transformed the meaning of life and the meaning of suffering. Although there are enemies of the cross, those who insist on living according to merely human values, Paul maintains that the cross will lead each Christian to eventual glory, because everyone who dies with Christ will share in his resurrection.[12] Naturally, this promise can be difficult to hold in view when one is actually undergoing an intense period of suffering, but it is nonetheless Paul's unwavering conviction about the ultimate meaning of the cross.

The cross is such a commonplace in our lives that we may have inadvertently allowed it to become an empty sign. We use the cross as jewelry in necklaces and earrings. But do the wearers know its meaning? We witness athletes crossing themselves before some final goal or basket or athletic contest, as if magically it will make them victorious. But do they understand its paradoxical message? And perhaps we rather absentmindedly sign ourselves with the cross going in and out of church, without really thinking about what this sign truly means.

As Paul insists, the cross should never be emptied of its profound meaning. The cross can never become a sign of "Christianity lite." There is no shortcut to authentic Christian life. Living the gospel is not easy. As Dietrich Bonhoeffer, the famous German theologian and martyr of the Nazi era taught, there is no such thing as "cheap grace." The cross is evidence that faith exacts a cost from those who would follow Christ. The cross is not a magical totem or a merely decorative item. For all who follow Jesus, it is the sign of true discipleship. It is

Paul's way of emphasizing Jesus' warning: "...whoever does not take up the cross and follow me is not worthy of me."[13] The cross is the sign of humbling oneself in order to surrender to the will of another, namely, God. The cross of Our Lord Jesus Christ will always remain a paradoxical sign in the world. It will always be a sign that invites ridicule and rejection. Yet it is the essential symbol of our faith. On this retreat we have the opportunity to renew our commitment to the cross. We surrender ourselves—body, mind and spirit—to the power of the cross.

To conclude this part of our conference, I suggest either singing or reciting the well-known traditional hymn, *Lift High the Cross*.[14]

Lift high the cross,
the love of Christ proclaim
till all the world adore
his sacred Name.

Come, brethren, follow where our Captain trod,
our King victorious, Christ the Son of God.

Led on their way by this triumphant sign,
the hosts of God in conquering ranks combine.

Each newborn soldier of the Crucified
bears on the brow the seal of him who died.
...
O Lord, once lifted on the glorious tree,
as thou hast promised, draw the world to thee.

FOR REFLECTION

Make your own list of "sufferings" that are a part of your life. How would you compare them to what Paul endured? Do you see them as a weakness? In what ways have they made you strong?

Read Psalm 22 slowly in front of a crucifix or a picture of the crucifixion. The first lines of this lament ("My God, my God, why have you forsaken me?") appear on Jesus' lips while he hangs on the cross.[15] Although they seem to be words of despair, they merely begin a lament psalm that ultimately expresses confidence in God's answer to prayer. How do you find these lines a comfort in the midst of trying times?

Do you ever feel that life is unfair and that you have received more than your share of suffering? How might Paul's approach to the cross of Jesus help you at such times?

When Paul prayed to have a mysterious difficulty (the "thorn in the side") removed from him, he says God responded, "My grace is sufficient for you, for power is made perfect in weakness" (2 Corinthians 12:9). Repeat this phrase over and over again, like a mantra, and meditate on its meaning.

Some readers may be familiar with the special Taizè ritual of "prayer around the cross." It originated with the ecumenical community in Taizè, France, and involves gathering around a cross, in a room illuminated by candles, and using readings and simple melodic chants to reflect on the mystery of the cross. If the retreat is being conducted in a group, this would be an appropriate service to use as a spiritual exercise following this conference.

CLOSING PRAYER

Heavenly Father, the mystery of suffering at times still challenges my faith to its very depth. I know that I am weak and that you are strong. I ask that you be merciful to me and to our world. I need your grace to transform my suffering into power, as your own Son did with the cross and as your servant Paul did in his ministry. Help me in my weakness, Lord. Do not let my fears, terrors and anxieties conquer me. Let me find that strength that you promise to those who suffer for the sake of righteousness, and let me boast only of the cross of your Son, Jesus Christ, in whose name I pray, and in the Holy Spirit, now and forever. Amen.

Notes

1. Mitch Albom, *Tuesdays with Morrie: An Old Man, A Young Man, and Life's Greatest Lesson* (New York: Broadway, 1997), pp. 150–151.
2. Job 3:1–3.
3. 2 Corinthians 11:23–33; author's translation.
4. 2 Corinthians 12:10.
5. Jeremiah 20:14.
6. Job 3:11.
7. See 1 Corinthians 4:16; 11:1.
8. Philippians 2:5–11, emphasis added.
9. See Romans 6:18–19; 1 Corinthians 9:19; Galatians 5:13; Ephesians 6:6.
10. The *New American Bible* translation makes this more explicit with the words "Because of this..." (Philippians 2:9).
11. Galatians 6:14.
12. See Philippians 3:8–12 and Romans 6:3–4.
13. Matthew 10:38.
14. The hymn is based upon a Pauline text, 1 Corinthians 1:18, and originated with George W. Kitchen (1827–1912) and Michael R. Newbolt (1874–1956). The Corinthian text reads: "For the message of the cross is foolishness to those who are perishing, but to us who are being saved it is the power of God" (author's translation).
15. Mark 15:34; Matthew 27:46.

DAY FOUR

LIVING
IN
THE
HOLY
SPIRIT

COMING TOGETHER IN THE SPIRIT

Several years ago, while attending a convention of educators, I heard a speaker tell the following story about a classroom experience that went something like this: A teacher was holding an art class for first graders. She told the children that they could draw anything they wanted, and she handed out paper and crayons to get them going. She then wandered about the classroom looking over the children's shoulders to observe their progress.

In a little while, she came upon a girl whose "picture" was very colorful but seemingly jumbled. Despite looking intently at the drawing for a few minutes, the teacher could not make out exactly what it represented, so she asked the girl, "What is that you're drawing, Rose?"

"A picture of God," came the quick response.

"Well, that is certainly an ambitious project. You do know, don't you, that no one knows what God looks like?" the teacher gently commented.

Without a moment's hesitation the little girl responded, "Well, they will now."

Probably few of us have the innocent boldness of the little girl to presume to know what God looks like. What is said about God, in general, is even truer about the Holy Spirit, in particular. Just how does one describe the Holy Spirit?

Traditionally in art, the Holy Spirit, the third person of the Blessed Trinity, is usually portrayed as a dove. This is an image based upon the description in the Gospels of the descent of the Holy Spirit upon Jesus at his baptism. Luke's Gospel makes the image concrete:

> Now when all the people were baptized, and when Jesus also had been baptized and was praying, the heaven was opened, and the Holy Spirit descended upon him in bodily form like a dove. And a voice came from heaven, "You are my Son, the Beloved; with you I am well pleased."[1]

We know intellectually, of course, that because God is a spirit, any physical description is simply our human attempt to put into vivid words and images what is more elusive. While it is true that no one knows what God looks like,[2] we have no choice but to try to describe God in human terms. Thus, the little girl in the story actually was not far off base at all. A series of multicolored lines and squiggles might be a very appropriate way to describe God on occasion, especially the Holy Spirit.

In today's retreat session, we will sit in prayer with the image of the Holy Spirit, using Saint Paul's letters for inspiration. We will invite the same Holy Spirit to come and be our guide in this process.

OPENING PRAYER
(to the Holy Spirit)
O Breath of the Father, sacred wind from heaven, come and breathe new life into me so that I may be renewed in my mind,

body and spirit as I make this retreat. Rekindle in me the spark of love that you placed there when I was baptized and confirmed. Replenish in me your holy gifts of wisdom, understanding, counsel, fortitude, knowledge, piety and fear of the Lord so that I might better serve all in holiness all my days. Intercede for me in times when I am too frail or weak to approach the throne of the Most High. Be my strength and my comfort, my advocate and my defender, for I seek always to be open to your promptings. In confidence, I pray to you now, with the love of the Father and the encouragement of the Son, forever and ever. Amen.

Retreat Session Four
Scriptures for Reflection

> But you are not in the flesh; you are in the Spirit, since the Spirit of God dwells in you. Anyone who does not have the Spirit of Christ does not belong to him. But if Christ is in you, though the body is dead because of sin, the Spirit is life because of righteousness. If the Spirit of him who raised Jesus from the dead dwells in you, he who raised Christ from the dead will give life to your mortal bodies also through his Spirit that dwells in you.... For all who are led by the Spirit of God are children of God. (Romans 8:9–11, 14)

> And God, who searches the heart, knows what is the mind of the Spirit, because the Spirit intercedes for the saints according to the will of God. (Romans 8:27)

> Now there are varieties of gifts, but the same Spirit; and there are varieties of services, but the same Lord; and there are varieties of activities, but it is the same God who

activates all of them in everyone. To each is given the
manifestation of the Spirit for the common good.
(1 Corinthians 12:4–7)

For most people, trying to comprehend the Holy Spirit is quite
challenging. How does one describe this invisible presence? It
is easier to identify and imagine God the Father and Jesus
Christ. Most people probably have a fairly detailed image in
their minds about the Father, perhaps influenced by artistic
portraits through the ages. This applies even more to the Son,
Jesus Christ, since there are countless portraits in art and literature to help us envision him. Jesus' very humanity makes it
easier for us both to identify him and identify *with* him. The
personhood of each of these figures is described in very
human fashion, using traditional masculine imagery. The
Holy Spirit is another matter.

Although the Holy Spirit will always remain a mysterious
and elusive reality, I will attempt to summarize Paul's main
teachings with four observations that I think can help focus
our reflection.

The first observation is that Paul shares with all the writers
of the New Testament a common background for the Holy
Spirit. They all understand the Holy Spirit to come from God.
Let's delve into this aspect in more detail.

Paul uses language that is familiar, rooted in the Old
Testament description of God's Spirit. Thus, the basic words
for the Spirit are also words that mean "breath" or "wind."[3]
Any attempt to get hold of the Spirit must wrestle with these
elusive realities. One cannot harness the wind in the sense of
holding it fast. Nor can one capture breath. They are very real
and can be felt and sometimes even seen. (Ever seen your

breath on a frosty morning?) Yet their effect is apparent. The wind can be destructive, as in a hurricane or a tornado, but it can also refresh, like on a hot summer's day. One's breath is so basic to life that it hardly needs emphasis. When breathing ceases, creatures die. The Holy Spirit, too, is basic to life, especially the "spiritual life." Without the Spirit, our interior lives wither. Indeed, spiritual life is nothing less than the life *of* the Spirit.

Paul is also quite clear that the Spirit is none other than God's Spirit. Nowhere in his letters does he attempt to describe the personality of the Holy Spirit, as if it were separate from God. He always views the Spirit as *God's* Spirit. God is the source.[4] The Spirit is like a divine force—a spiritual engine, a divine power, if you will—that makes all life go. God infuses the Spirit throughout the whole of the cosmos. (Remember God's "Spirit" hovering over the chaos at creation?)[5] Most importantly, God places the human "spirit" in each human being. (Remember God "breathing into" Adam the breath of life?)[6] God gives each person God's own Spirit. This means that our destiny is always otherworldly. God created us for an ultimate destiny that is truly spiritual, because it emanates from and returns to God. As Paul says to the Philippians, "[O]ur citizenship is in heaven, and it is from there that we are expecting a Savior, the Lord Jesus Christ."[7] We are destined therefore to be citizens of another realm and to enjoy the fullness of life promised by the Holy Spirit.

Just as important is Paul's understanding that the Holy Spirit is closely tied to Jesus Christ. The Spirit is not only God's Spirit, but also Christ's.[8] In fact, we might say that the Holy Spirit completes the circle of love inherently present in God's own being. The Spirit comes from God the Father, but also is united to Christ. The Spirit is associated with the works of Christ and also with his suffering, death and resurrection. The Spirit becomes another way in which the risen Christ continues to work in this world and among those who believe in him. Indeed, only by means of the Holy Spirit is one able to cry out in faith, "Jesus is Lord."[9] The Holy Spirit is thus an enabler, leading us to take the leap of faith in Christ. While we remain on this earth, Christ's Spirit animates all that we do and gives us the ability to follow Christ's example of a life of service to others.

In essence, then, Paul's thought expresses a truly trinitarian understanding of God. This is a vital "mystery" of our faith. The Father, the Son and the Holy Spirit are intimately related; they are one. In fact, he expresses this truth with a liturgical formula in a passage that we have adapted as a greeting in the Mass: "The grace of the Lord Jesus Christ, the love of God, and the fellowship of the Holy Spirit be with all of you!"[10]

The second observation about Paul's notion of the Holy Spirit focuses on the effect of the Spirit upon believers. Let's flesh out this idea.

Paul confidently asserts that the Holy Spirit dwells in believers. We are in fact a temple of the Holy Spirit. He boldly asks the Corinthians, "Do you not know that you are God's temple and that God's Spirit dwells in you?"[11] The Holy Spirit finds a home in our very being. Lest we think of this only in some sort of otherworldly fashion, some supernatural way, Paul reminds the Corinthians that their very bodies are the site of this indwelling. God places the Spirit within us here and now, in our earthly existence. Each of us has a "spirit" (small *s*) marked by the Spirit (capital *S*). Becoming "spiritual" is not merely awaiting a heavenly existence. The Spirit functions within us in our physical being because, as Paul says, "God's love has been poured into our hearts through the Holy Spirit that has been given to us."[12] Elsewhere he warns the Ephesians that they should not grieve this indwelling Holy Spirit by actions that betray their destiny. He says, "[D]o not grieve the Holy Spirit of God, with which you were marked with a seal for the day of redemption."[13] Since they are temples of the Holy Spirit, ultimately destined for redemption and for glory, all they are and all they do should reflect this reality.

Paul further explains that this gift of God comes in power and is mediated through the waters of baptism. The Spirit does not arrive in a whimsy. The Spirit is always purposeful and comes in power. Paul reminds the Thessalonians of this reality specifically, recalling the time when he preached the gospel message in their midst and they received it in power and the Holy Spirit in a convincing manner.

> For we know, brothers and sisters beloved by God, that he has chosen you, because our message of the gospel came to you not in word only, but also in power and in the Holy Spirit and with full conviction; just as you know what kind of persons we proved to be among you for your sake.[14]

The reception of the Holy Spirit, then, is an empowerment mediated by the baptismal waters and the gift of faith. In the Letter to Titus, Paul explicitly calls attention to "the water of rebirth and renewal by the Holy Spirit."[15] The Spirit leads to renewal, power and conviction. That is why, in part, each session of our retreat has begun with a section entitled, "Coming Together in the Spirit." The Spirit drives our focus, gives us strength to persevere and accompanies us on our spiritual journey.

Furthermore, Paul understands the Holy Spirit to be the primary means of sanctification for believers. We mentioned on the first day of the retreat that God wills our holiness—sanctification. Paul reminds the Corinthians, "But you were washed, you were sanctified, you were justified in the name of the Lord Jesus Christ and in the Spirit of our God."[16] And he says to the Thessalonians,

> But we must always give thanks to God for you, brothers and sisters beloved by the Lord, because God chose you as the first fruits for salvation through sanctification by the Spirit and through belief in the truth.[17]

Yet sanctification, while it begins on earth, is not completed here. It ultimately finds its fulfillment in the kingdom of God. The Holy Spirit is always leading us further along in our journey toward holiness and, eventually, to the kingdom of God. Because we cannot achieve this goal on our own, the Holy Spirit is God's gift of accompaniment. The Spirit walks with us, leads us onward, guides us on the path.

A third and well-known observation about Paul's understanding of the Holy Spirit concerns the "gifts" that are apparent in the community of faith. The Holy Spirit is the source of all these gifts. Let's look at this idea in more detail.

Paul's eloquent passage in 1 Corinthians is the most obvious place to reflect on this point of the mystery of the Spirit. Paul writes at length about the diversity of gifts in the community, the church. This makes for a dramatic reflection on the mystery of the diversity of gifts and the oneness of their source. An excerpt of the passage was quoted at the beginning of this conference; here is the longer citation.

> Now there are varieties of gifts, but the same Spirit; and there are varieties of services, but the same Lord; and there are varieties of activities, but it is the same God who activates all of them in everyone. To each is given the manifestation of the Spirit for the common good. To one is given through the Spirit the utterance of wisdom, and to another the utterance of knowledge according to the same Spirit, to another faith by the same Spirit, to another gifts of healing by the one Spirit, to another the working of miracles, to another prophecy, to another the discernment of spirits, to another various kinds of tongues, to another the interpretation of tongues. All these are activated by one and the same Spirit, who allots to each one individually just as the Spirit chooses. For just as the body is one and has many members, and all the members of the body, though many, are one body, so it is with Christ. For in the one Spirit we were all baptized into one body—Jews or Greeks, slaves or free.[18]

In this passage, Paul is at one and the same time commending the individual members of the community for their unique gifts—of which they are no doubt proud—but also reminding them that the one and only Holy Spirit is their source. The gifts come to individuals, but they are intended for the entire church. The Holy Spirit bestows these gifts precisely to help build up the community, "for the common good." And notice the breadth of the gifts. When one keeps the whole of 1 Corinthians 12 in view, the gifts are broad-ranging. They include ministries in word and in deed, in prophecy and interpretation, in preaching and teaching, in evangelizing and administration. One could rightly say that there are as many gifts as there are people. Each of us has been given a unique identity and possesses gifts that suit us perfectly.

Finally, the fourth observation about Paul's notion of the Holy Spirit concerns the verification of the work of the Spirit among us. In reality, this notion leads to a question that not only Paul, but every subsequent Christian, has had to ask: How does one know that you are living in the Holy Spirit? Paul answers the question with a reminder that addressing it requires discernment.[19]

Discernment relies on evidence. Likely, you learned in your catechism instruction that, just as there are gifts of the Holy Spirit, so there are "fruits" of the Spirit. Paul concretizes them in this fashion:

> ...the fruit of the Spirit is love, joy, peace, patience, kindness, generosity, faithfulness, gentleness, and self-control.... If we live by the Spirit, let us also be guided by the Spirit.[20]

This passage, in fact, is the basis of the church's teaching about the twelve fruits of the Holy Spirit. The *Catechism of the Catholic Church* lists them as: charity, joy, peace, patience, kindness, goodness, generosity, gentleness, faithfulness, modesty, self-control and chastity.[21] But note that Paul uses the singular expression "fruit." He does not view these virtues as separate attitudes or actions. Rather, they represent a unified way of living in the Holy Spirit. In essence, one "fruit" flows out of life in the Holy Spirit that shows itself in a multiplicity of ways. One's entire life, filled with thoughts, words, attitudes and actions, points to evidence of life in the Spirit.

Bearing the fruit of the Spirit means living according to the Spirit's desire and power. The expression "to bear fruit" is a common biblical image in both the Old and New Testaments to describe how one lives one's life. As Jesus once said, "Thus you will know them by their fruits."[22] One cannot simply say, "I am living in the Holy Spirit." One should be able to point to one's way of life and say, "See how I live in the Holy Spirit." In other words, there is an ethical dimension to life in the Spirit, which we will explore in more depth in our sixth retreat session. Surrendering to this spiritual power shows forth in righteous attitudes, holy thoughts and words, and good deeds. These are the fruit of the Spirit.

So what does Paul instruct us about living in the Holy Spirit in these four observations? Rather than painting a picture or telling a story, Paul calls his readers to raise their sights. They should look upward, inward and forward to encounter the Spirit. Remember that God is the source. God has planted within you his own Holy Spirit. You are a temple. You have an internal compass to guide you on the path that leads to true sanctity and, in the end, to the kingdom. And this Spirit has provided you unique gifts—talents, if you will—that are to be used to promote harmony in the community. Living in the Spirit means putting your gifts to good use for others. The community of faith will help discern your authentic gifts, and your thoughts, words and deeds will verify that you are indeed possessed by the breath of the Spirit.

In short, living in the Spirit is ultimately entrusting your life to God's power and being led along a path that is righteous and true. It is God's grace at work in our lives day after day.

FOR REFLECTION

Read Galatians 5:18–25, where Paul contrasts "the works of the flesh" with the fruit of the Holy Spirit. Both lists are quite concrete. Can you identity any qualities on the lists that are operative in your life? What "fruit" have you borne in your life? Make a prayer to the Holy Spirit in your own words asking to have your life bear fruit that reflects the life of the Spirit planted within you.

In 1 Thessalonians 5:19 Paul writes: "Do not quench the Spirit." What do you think he means by this expression? How is it possible to quench the Holy Spirit? What qualities or attitudes would work against quenching the Spirit?

For Catholics especially, the sacrament of confirmation is most associated with receiving the Holy Spirit in a way that "confirms" the faith professed at baptism. Confirmation is meant to signal an "adult" type of faith, a conscious decision to live the faith. Review your own commitment of faith at this stage of your life. In what ways have you lived out the expectations set forth at your confirmation? In what ways do you need to strengthen your commitment? Has your life in the Spirit grown over time?

Paul writes in Romans 8:15–16, "When we cry, 'Abba! Father!' it is that very Spirit bearing witness with our spirit that we are children of God." Pray the Our Father, the prayer Jesus taught his disciples, slowly and meditatively, consciously calling on the aid of the Holy Spirit to strengthen your relationship to God as a loving Father. Remember that the Spirit will accompany you in your prayer.

If you are artistically inclined, why not imitate the little girl in the opening story? You may just hit upon the right combination of colors and images that mirror the multifaceted reality of the Holy Spirit in your life.

CLOSING PRAYER

As the final prayer for this retreat conference, I suggest recalling a traditional hymn[23] to the Holy Spirit (under the older designation, Holy Ghost), which can be sung or recited:

Come, Holy Ghost, Creator Blest,
And in our hearts take up Thy rest;
Come with thy grace and heav'nly aid,
To fill the hearts which Thou hast made,
To fill the hearts which Thou hast made.

O Comforter Blest, to thee we cry,
Thou heav'nly gift of God most high;
Thou font of life and fire of love,
And sweet anointing from above,
And sweet anointing from above.

Praise be to Thee Father and Son,
And Holy Spirit Three in one;
And may the Son on us bestow
The gifts that from the Spirit flow,
The gifts that from the Spirit flow.

Notes

1. Luke 3:21–22. Matthew and Mark also refer to the descent of the Spirit "like a dove," but Luke emphasizes that it was in "bodily form." Compare Matthew 3:16 and Mark 1:10.
2. When John 1:18 says, "No one has ever seen God," it means that no one can know what God looks like in reality.

3. The Hebrew word *(ruach)* and the Greek word *(pneuma)* have essentially the same root idea, meaning "wind" or "breath." The Latin translation of the Bible uses the word *spiritus* with the same root meaning from which the English words *spirit, inspiration, inspired* and so on derive. Thus all these languages preserve the multiple root meanings of the expression.

4. 1 Thessalonians 4:8 explicitly says that God gives the Holy Spirit.

5. Genesis 1:1, translated by the NRSV as "a wind from God" and by *The New American Bible* as "a mighty wind."

6. Genesis 2:7.

7. Philippians 3:20.

8. See Romans 8:9; Galatians 4:6.

9. 1 Corinthians 12:3.

10. 2 Corinthians 13:13, author's translation.

11. 1 Corinthians 3:16.

12. Romans 5:5.

13. Ephesians 4:30.

14. 1 Thessalonians 1:4–5.

15. Titus 3:5.

16. 1 Corinthians 6:11.

17. 2 Thessalonians 2:13.

18. 1 Corinthians 12:4–13.

19. Romans 12:2; notice that 1 Corinthians 12:10 shows discernment itself as one of the gifts of the Holy Spirit.

20. Galatians 5:22–25. See also Romans 14:17 and 1 Thessalonians 1:6 where Paul mentions righteousness, peace, joy and love that flow from the Holy Spirit.

21. *Catechism of the Catholic Church*, second edition (Rome: Libreria Editrice Vaticana, 2000), #1832. This list is based upon the Latin Vulgate form of Galatians 5:22–23.

22. Matthew 7:20. See also Matthew 7:16–18; Psalm 1:1–3; Isaiah 3:10; and Jeremiah 32:19 for some other passages using "fruit" or "fruits" as an image for the deeds of one's life.

23. The original Latin text, *Veni, Creator Spiritus*, is attributed to Rabanus Maurus (AD 776–856). The translation for this particular form of the hymn was done by Edward Caswall (1814–1878).

DAY FIVE

LEARNING

TO

PRAY

WITHOUT

CEASING

COMING TOGETHER IN THE SPIRIT

William Shakespeare has captured in poetic fashion the experience that many people encounter when they try to pray:

> Pray can I not,
> Though inclination be as sharp as will:
> My stronger guilt defeats my strong intent;
> And, like a man to double business bound,
> I stand in pause where I shall first begin.[1]

Just where does one begin in prayer? One thing is sure: if one is uncertain about how to pray, this should not become an absolute stumbling block. Paul had his own take on the predicament:

> Likewise the Spirit helps us in our weakness; for we do not know how to pray as we ought, but that very Spirit intercedes with sighs too deep for words.[2]

For Paul, God provides, by means of the Holy Spirit, a way to pray. Even when we are at a loss for words, even when we think we do not know how to pray, the Holy Spirit supplies what we lack in our method, through "sighs too deep for words." These miraculous groanings of the Holy Spirit are God's way of initiating the dialogue that we are so desperate to have. That is why this conference follows closely on the heels of the previous one, which focused on the Holy Spirit.

All retreats are an opportunity to hone our prayer lives. They offer an invitation to sit quietly and await the rekindling of a dialogue between God and ourselves. On this fifth day of our retreat, we concentrate on the power of prayer. We seek to jump-start our prayer life that perhaps, with even the best of intentions, has become tired, worn out or stale. Even in times of frustration that the quality of our prayer does not seem to match some pre-established standard, Paul reminds us that the Holy Spirit is there intervening on our behalf. Let us trust in that Spirit to teach us once more to pray from the depths of our heart.

OPENING PRAYER

Lord, I know not where to begin, nor do I know exactly what to say. Help my hesitation. Place your words in my mouth, for you know my thoughts even before I speak them. Send me your Holy Spirit to be my instructor. Search my heart and release my deepest yearnings and my darkest fears so that I might place them before you and receive your mercy. Teach me patience in this process, for I await your word and I am open to your will. In Jesus' name and in the Spirit, I pray now and forever. Amen.

RETREAT SESSION FIVE

Scriptures for Reflection

> Rejoice always, pray without ceasing, give thanks in all circumstances: for this is the will of God in Christ Jesus for you. (1 Thessalonians 5:16–18)

> Rejoice in hope, be patient in suffering, persevere in prayer. (Romans 12:12)

> I thank my God every time I remember you, constantly praying with joy in every one of my prayers for all of you, because of your sharing in the gospel from the first day until now. (Philippians 1:3–5)

Everyone knows that prayer is essentially a dialogue that grows out of a relationship. The *Catechism of the Catholic Church* devotes a large section to Christian prayer. At the beginning of that section, the *Catechism* draws attention to prayer as gift, covenant and communion.[3] In other words, God provides the starting point. Prayer begins with God reaching out to human beings. It involves an invitation to a covenantal relationship, to entering into communion with the One who brought us into being. Prayer is thus not simply a human exercise. It is an integral part of a divine dance, a give and take with a God who desires to be closer to us than we are to ourselves.

Paul would understand and affirm this description of prayer. He talks about prayer more than any other writer in the New Testament, mentioning it through a variety of expressions more than one hundred times in the thirteen letters. Prayer was obviously important for Paul.

What does he say about it? I will summarize Paul's understanding by means of eight observations that I think can be useful for our reflections.

First, Paul knows that prayer is not always easy. That is why he says God sometimes provides the guidance needed in prayer, as quoted earlier: "Likewise the Spirit helps us in our weakness; for we do not know how to pray as we ought, but that very Spirit intercedes with sighs too deep for words."[4] Sometimes prayer is simply surrendering to this loving gesture by the Holy Spirit when we can't pray on our own. I remember once hearing the late Cardinal Joseph Bernardin of Chicago giving advice to seminarians and priests in a talk about the need to pray when you feel well. He lamented that when he was very sick with the cancer that eventually took his life, he really did not have the strength to pray as he wanted. His attempts to formulate prayers were weak, just as his body was weak from the disease. In such times, the Holy Spirit makes up for what is lacking in our own spirit and flesh. This is why prayer is a gift from God, not simply a human activity. God created us, and prayer flows out of being creatures of this loving Creator.

Second, Paul emphasizes the importance of thanksgiving in prayer. In fact, all of his letters, save Galatians, contain sections of thanksgiving prayers immediately after the opening of the letter.[5] Prayer is always an act of gratitude. Paul understands that we should never restrict prayers to supplication or petition alone. Prayer should be an act of giving thanks to God. Paul frequently uses the language of thanksgiving in his letters, even in the ones written from prison (like Philippians or Ephesians). Paul's attitude in prayer is one of continual thanksgiving, often for blessings bestowed, but most frequently for the gift of his communities of faith and their acceptance of his message.[6] His thanksgiving is frequently tinged with joy, for joy is a proper attitude for the Christian, even in the midst of suffering or heartache. For example, Paul writes to the Philippians:

> But even if I am being poured out as a libation over the sacrifice and the offering of your faith, I am glad and rejoice with all of you—and in the same way you also must be glad and rejoice with me.[7]

Thus, thanksgiving and joy naturally go together in prayer and show our proper attitude to God for everything that comes our way.

Third, prayer is a spiritual activity that can carry us beyond this world and put us in touch with the kingdom of God. This is another way of saying that prayer is also a mystical activity. It places us in touch with God's mysterious Spirit, and sometimes in prayer we experience being "in another world," as it were, when we are drawn more and more into the mystery of God. Paul describes what many scholars believe is his own experience of mystical prayer in the following way:

> I know a person in Christ who fourteen years ago was caught up to the third heaven—whether in the body or out of the body I do not know; God knows. And I know that such a person—whether in the body or out of the body I do not know; God knows—was caught up into Paradise and heard things that are not to be told, that no mortal is permitted to repeat.[8]

This may well be Paul's description of his call from the risen Lord Jesus on the road to Damascus. In any case, Paul is speaking of a remarkable experience of being in God's presence (in Paradise, he says) in a manner that he can scarcely describe in words. Indeed, it was a revelation that he cannot repeat to others. If one is sometimes drawn into such mystical experiences, it is a true grace.

Fourth, Paul's most frequent use of prayer language is in supplication for others, especially his beloved communities.[9] He often reminds his communities about how earnestly and regularly he and his colleagues pray for them. Prayer is often a request. Prayers of supplication are part of the dialogue. We literally ask God to bless others, to provide for their needs and to heal their hurts. It is thus not a bad thing that much of our prayer life would be spent in petition for those who are dear to us. Little wonder that the "prayers of the faithful" that we offer at Mass are usually petitions. To ask God's hearing for the needs of our church and our world is an act of faith. The very gesture of such prayers of supplication means that we believe God cares about us. He invites us into a covenant, into communion with him. God wants what is good for us. God can hear and is willing to answer our prayers. Our needs and deepest desires are of interest to God. God can be moved with pity, even if the answer we receive is not always exactly what we had in mind.

But Paul does not restrict prayers of supplication to others. A fifth aspect of his teachings on prayer is his request of his communities that they pray for him.[10] This may at first strike us as a bit self-serving. It might be bad enough if we thought Paul constantly prayed for himself, but how much more selfish would it be to invite others' prayers for him? But for Paul, inviting the prayers of others for oneself is not a selfish act. Instead, it is an act of humility. It means that he acknowledges he does not have all the answers, nor does he have all the strength to keep going without assistance. Prayers of supplication for himself and his coworkers, he believed, could help him and his colleagues fulfill their duties as bearers of the gospel of Jesus Christ. So we should likewise not be bashful about inviting others to pray for us.

Despite such rare and precious occurrences, Paul also urges that prayer in the Spirit does not mean we should ignore active mental prayer. This is my sixth point. As desirable and rewarding as otherworldly experiences are, for most of us prayer is a more mundane experience. It is a conscious mental activity. It can be easy to exaggerate the more exciting, charismatic experiences of prayer and forget the more common everyday experience. Paul had to warn some in Corinth that they were being carried away with the more charismatic aspects of prayer in the context of "speaking in tongues" while forgetting that prayer is also an activity of the mind. (I recall one speaker humorously describing the Corinthians' attraction to charismatic prayer as having swallowed the Holy Spirit, feathers and all!) Paul wrote:

> Therefore, one who speaks in a tongue should pray for the power to interpret. For if I pray in a tongue, my spirit prays but my mind is unproductive. What should I do then? I will pray with the spirit, but I will pray with the mind also; I will sing praise with the spirit, but I will sing praise with the mind also.[11]

At times I have known people who judge the quality of prayer by its emotional impact. They seek out such experiences and make them normative for everyone else. This has occasionally happened with very moving retreat experiences, engaged encounters, Cursillos, charismatic prayer meetings and the like. Paul offers a reminder that good as these experiences are, they should not blind us to the more common prayer experiences. In other words, don't let the inability to achieve an emotional high in prayer deceive you. Prayer takes place in a range of human emotions.

The seventh observation concerns the simplicity of Christian prayer. When it comes to prayer forms, Paul also exhibits the characteristic knowledge of the teaching of Jesus. You will remember that when his disciples asked Jesus to teach them to pray, he responded with the Our Father, which we call "the Lord's Prayer."[12] In contrast to the lengthy and showy prayers of some of his contemporaries, Jesus' model of prayer is brief, humble, intimate and to the point. In Matthew's Gospel, this prayer is the centerpiece of the Sermon on the Mount, and it quickly became the identification badge of all Christians. It was also the way Jesus himself prayed: "Abba, Father."[13] Paul, too, used this prayer, and we can rightly assume that his communities regularly prayed this simple prayer, which has become the model Christian prayer for all time.[14]

Finally, the eighth point is that Paul reminds his readers that prayer is neither an optional nor an occasional activity for Christians. Prayer should be a constant in our lives. He explicitly mentions that he prays constantly, and he urges his communities to do likewise.[15] But in this advice, a practical question arises. What constitutes "praying always" or praying "without ceasing"?

One danger in taking this advice literally is that we simply say, "my life is my prayer" or "my work is my prayer" or "in everything I do, I am always praying." We should not deceive ourselves that prayer is simply dedicating our day to God. Prayer is a conscious activity. It is actively reflecting on God's presence. Paul does not define what he means when he advises us to pray always, but one gets the sense from his letters that prayer was a daily activity and was never far from his mind, his lips and his heart. Although he was certainly busy as a missionary, prayer was a part of his everyday routine. It was his way of bringing God into everything he was about. As a faithful Jew and a Pharisee, daily prayer would have been a normal part of the rhythm of his day. Prayer punctuated the key hours of the day. Paul no doubt transferred this practice into his exercise of prayer once he accepted Jesus as the Messiah. But I think there is even more to Paul's desire always to be at prayer. Let me give an example from later Christian tradition.

In the late seventeenth century, a humble French Carmelite by the name of Brother Lawrence of the Resurrection wrote a series of reflections that came to be collected and known as *The Practice of the Presence of God*.[16] This was no great spiritual tract in comparison to many other publications of the mystics, but his simple spiritual advice captivated the imagination of his contemporaries. Despite the many menial tasks that he was required to do as a brother, such as sweeping, cleaning, preparing meals and so on, he developed a way of consciously calling to mind God's presence even in the midst of these mundane activities. It required patience and perseverance, but little by little he grew in holiness by means of short, simple conversations with God in the midst of his daily chores.

While I am not suggesting Brother Lawrence took his inspiration directly from Saint Paul, I believe his little treatise, which has gained in popularity in recent decades, captures the spirit of what Paul meant. Praying unceasingly is cultivating the presence of God day in and day out in ordinary life. To achieve it one must be patient but also persevering. Just as any friendship requires time and presence in order for it to flourish, so does our relationship with God. Spending time with God, in silence and in vocal prayer, helps to foster the relationship. It is the key to praying unceasingly. In Paul, we have an example of one who mastered this prayer form in his daily life and who urged his communities to do likewise.

I should emphasize as we draw this conference to a close that Paul never attempted a systematic study on prayers. He does not offer a total analysis of prayer. There is much in the Christian tradition after Paul, especially among the mystics, like Teresa of Avila, John of the Cross, Ignatius Loyola, Edith Stein and others, who offer many more deep insights.

Yet we can say that Paul understood prayer to be central to the spiritual life. He had a rich and varied prayer life that included personal prayer (supplication, thanksgiving and reflecting on the Scriptures), liturgical prayer (sacraments like baptism, Eucharist and reconciliation) and mystical prayer (speaking in tongues and prophecy). While Paul did not say everything about prayer that might be helpful today, what he does say is fundamental to our understanding. Prayer is very much at the heart of the life of faith. It keeps us open to God's presence and action in the world. It also provides the main avenue to speak to God from the depths of our being. In this eternal dialogue, our spiritual life grows and is sustained—

precisely what we are looking for on a retreat.

I will conclude this retreat session with a lengthier quotation from the Letter to the Ephesians. It contains one of the most beautiful prayers in the New Testament. In it Paul prays intensely for his community. He expresses his deepest desire that they be drawn into the presence of God in such a profound way that they will actually *know* in all their being just how incredibly mysterious and loving God is. Although this is Paul's prayer for the Ephesians, it can also become our prayer for those who are dear to us.

> I pray therefore that you may not lose heart over my sufferings for you; they are your glory. For this reason I bow my knees before the Father, from whom every family in heaven and on earth takes its name. I pray that, according to the riches of his glory, he may grant that you may be strengthened in your inner being with power through his Spirit, and that Christ may dwell in your hearts through faith, as you are being rooted and grounded in love. I pray that you may have the power to comprehend, with all the saints, what is the breadth and length and height and depth, and to know the love of Christ that surpasses knowledge, so that you may be filled with all the fullness of God. Now to him who by the power at work within us is able to accomplish abundantly far more than all we can ask or imagine, to him be glory in the church and in Christ Jesus to all generations, forever and ever. Amen.[17]

FOR REFLECTION

Read Romans 15:30–33, Paul's plea for prayers from the Romans on his behalf. Asking for people's prayers for yourself is not selfish. It is an act of faith in both God and the ones you love. When was the last time you humbly asked others to pray for you?

Read Philemon 4–6, Paul's prayer for his friend and fellow believer Philemon, for whom he gives thanks. Call to mind quietly in prayer those of your own personal circle of family, friends, coworkers and colleagues upon whom you ask God's special blessing.

Sit quietly for fifteen minutes, not trying to speak to God or attempting to formulate any specific prayers. Just listen carefully. Does God speak to you? Allow the Holy Spirit to provide your inspiration.

Read Romans 10:1, Paul's prayer for the salvation of Israel. Paul regularly prays for those who are not believers in Jesus Christ. Spend some time in prayer for those in our own day who are not believers.

CLOSING PRAYER

Gracious and loving God, I thank you for your presence and action in my life. I praise and glorify your name for teaching me the path of prayer, for setting my heart to your own. I freely acknowledge my weaknesses but I surrender them totally to you. Take my humble prayers—for my family, my friends, my colleagues, my parish, myself and even my enemies—and shape them into an acceptable offering. Hear and answer me when I call upon you, for I always trust in your goodness, and I will never allow myself to lose sight of your faithful presence. In the name of Jesus, and in the Holy Spirit, I pray. Amen.

Notes

1. *Hamlet,* Act 3, scene 3, lines 38–42.
2. Romans 8:26.
3. *Catechism of the Catholic Church,* second edition (Rome: Libreria Editrice Vaticana, 2000), #2559–2565.
4. Romans 8:26.
5. See Galatians 1:1–6. Paul is so upset with the Galatians that he launches right away into his concern about their abandonment of the gospel, bypassing the usual prayer of thanksgiving.
6. Philippians 4:6; 1 Thessalonians 1:2; 1 Timothy 2:1.
7. Philippians 2:17–18.
8. 2 Corinthians 12:2–4.
9. For example, Romans 1:9; 10:1; 2 Corinthians 9:14; 13:9.
10. For example, Romans 15:30; 2 Corinthians 1:11; 1 Thessalonians 5:25; Ephesians 6:19; Philemon 22.
11. 1 Corinthians 14:13–15.
12. See Matthew 6:9–15 and Luke 11:1–4.
13. Mark 14:36.
14. See Romans 8:15 and Galatians 4:6. The word *abba* is an intimate Aramaic word for "father," something akin to "Dad." Scholars are generally agreed that the word expresses Jesus' intimacy with his heavenly Father. The fact that Jesus taught his disciples to pray in like manner indicates his desire to share this intimate relationship with his followers.
15. See Philippians 1:4; Colossians 1:9; 4:2; 1 Thessalonians 5:17.
16. See John J. Delaney, trans., *The Practice of the Presence of God, by Brother Lawrence of the Resurrection* (New York: Doubleday, 1977).
17. Ephesians 3:15–21.

DAY SIX

LEADING THE VIRTUOUS LIFE: FAITH, HOPE AND LOVE

COMING TOGETHER IN THE SPIRIT

During a lecture series that I was giving on the theology of Saint Paul, a participant came up to me and told the following joke that he had apparently picked up off the Internet.

A man died and went to heaven and was met at the "pearly gates" by Saint Peter. Saint Peter informed him: "Here are the rules. You have to get 100 points to make it into heaven. So you tell me all the good things you did in your life, and I'll keep score. You get a certain number of points for each good deed. When you reach one hundred, you're in."

"Okay," the man responded. "I was married to the same woman for more than fifty years, and I was always faithful to her, even in my heart."

"Great," said Saint Peter, "that's worth three points."

"Three points?" the man said in reply, a bit concerned.

"Well," he went on, "I attended church every Sunday and always supported the church's ministry by tithing and volunteering."

"Great," came the response back, "that's certainly worth a point."

"Only one point!?!" said the man, now quite worried for his immortal soul.

"Well, I started a soup kitchen in my city and worked in a shelter for homeless people."

"Fantastic, that's worth another two points," came the reply.

"Two points!" the man cried out, clearly exasperated. "At that rate, the only way I'll get to heaven is by the grace of God!!"

Saint Peter smiles and nods his head. "Bingo! 100 points! Come on in."

This humorous story makes an important point that is consistent with Paul's outlook. Salvation is God's free gift to humankind. Jesus made the one supreme sacrifice that saved all people. God's grace alone ensures our salvation, not our good deeds.

This assertion, of course, raises a troubling question for many people: Then why do we do good deeds at all? If they have little bearing on whether we "get into heaven," or just how "high up" we go, what is the purpose of good deeds? On this day of our retreat we will reflect in more depth on why the virtuous life is, indeed, still necessary for all who follow Jesus Christ.

OPENING PRAYER

Have mercy on me, Lord, a sinner. I place myself in your hands and ask that you mold me in your own image. Make of me an upright person, one who keeps your lawful commands and honors your will night and day. I seek to improve my life on this retreat, but I know that I can only accomplish this with your grace and your love. When I fall, help me to get up. When I fail, strengthen my resolve to try again. And when I succeed, fill me with joy. I place all that I am at your disposal. Teach me to say, "Thy will be done," as your Son once taught, and then accomplished by the wood of the cross. In his name and in the Holy Spirit, I pray. Amen.

RETREAT SESSION SIX

Scriptures for Reflection

> Paul, Silvanus, and Timothy, to the church of the Thessalonians in God the Father and the Lord Jesus Christ: Grace to you and peace. We always give thanks to God for all of you and mention you in our prayers, constantly remembering before our God and Father your work of faith and labor of love and steadfastness of hope in our Lord Jesus Christ. (1 Thessalonians 1:1–3)

> When I was a child, I spoke like a child, I thought like a child, I reasoned like a child; when I became an adult, I put an end to childish ways. For now we see in a mirror, dimly, but then we will see face to face. Now I know only in part; then I will know fully, even as I have been fully known. And now faith, hope, and love abide, these three; and the greatest of these is love. (1 Corinthians 13:11–13)

> Brothers and sisters, join in imitating me, and observe those who live according to the example you have in us. (Philippians 3:17)

I find it interesting that Paul sometimes uses the image of the child in his letters. Perhaps he remembered that Jesus had taught,

> Truly I tell you, unless you change and become like children, you will never enter the kingdom of heaven. Whoever becomes humble like this child is the greatest in the kingdom of heaven.[1]

This image is quite startling in that it goes against our natural tendencies. We think the goal of life is to grow up, to mature. Yet Jesus called his disciples to become like children. This, of course, did not mean to become childish. Rather, it means to become childlike—to be free, innocent, inquisitive, humble and able to be molded in the form of the parents. As beautiful and striking as this image is, it is not generally what Paul means when he invokes the image of children.

Paul's use of the image is perhaps more of what we normally expect. There is a time to be a child, but there is also a time to be an adult. He admits that he was at one time "childish," we might say, in his faith. When he grew up or matured in faith, he finally embraced all that faith demanded. He became an "adult" believer. He was mature in Christ.

He often compared himself to a parent who had to remind his communities, his "children," that they sometimes needed disciplining because of failures to live up to the standards of the gospel message he had preached. To the Corinthians, for example, he spoke about their lack of readiness to assume adult responsibilities.

And so, brothers and sisters, I could not speak to you as spiritual people, but rather as people of the flesh, as infants in Christ. I fed you with milk, not solid food, for you were not ready for solid food. Even now you are still not ready, for you are still of the flesh. For as long as there is jealousy and quarreling among you, are you not of the flesh, and behaving according to human inclinations?[2]

I should probably say a word here about Paul's contrast of spirit and flesh that appears in this passage and elsewhere in his letters. The flesh is not an expression restricted to sexual sins; it refers, rather, to the finite limitation of all human existence. Living "in the flesh" or as "people of the flesh," then, means living in a strictly human fashion. It encompasses all that is fleeting, limited and does not endure forever. In contrast, living "in the Spirit" or as "spiritual people" means living according to God's ways. It is focusing on the things that have lasting value and will endure forever. For Paul these are two overarching categories of the ethical life. Obviously, he exhorts his people toward the one and not the other. He wants them to live according to God's values, not human values. He asks them to set their sights on higher things (spiritual life, which is "above") rather than the lower things of human existence (fleshly life, which is "below"). Thus, for Paul, the life of the flesh does not mean improper sexual activities, exclusively, although they are part of the reality. (Sexual preoccupation, after all, was a reality in his day as much as it is today, especially in port cities like Corinth.) Instead, Paul calls his communities to be "spiritual" and not "fleshly" people.

In the passage above, using this traditional contrast, Paul reprimands the Corinthians for not living the way they should. (Remember, the real problem in Corinth was the divisions within the community.) They are being seduced by a merely human perspective rather than living according to a truly spiritual perspective. Their faith has not matured. They are like infants—not ready for solid food! They are not yet grown up enough to embody the true spiritual life.

I realize that for readers who are parents, especially of young children, this may come as a surprise. After all, parents naturally instruct their children in the faith from the very earliest years. The church even expects that parents will do this, teaching their children the basics of the faith, showing them how to pray and reading Bible stories to them. All of this, of course, is done in a manner that befits children, with simple words and illustrations. This is still appropriate. Paul is not railing against any such practices.

But for Paul, Christian faith was not child's play. It was serious, adult business. If for a time, the faith must be explained in simple terms, there comes a moment when every follower of Jesus Christ must step forward and put childish things behind. One's faith is meant to mature. Each Christian is called to act in adult fashion. This means putting into action the ethical ideals that flow from the gospel message. The virtues are necessary not to gain God's approval or to earn salvation but to demonstrate that the salvation that has been accomplished in Jesus is indeed at work in our lives. Leading ethically upright lives shows the world that we are followers of Jesus Christ. Our good deeds illustrate that we have put the gospel into action. They demonstrate our faith at work. Although God has bestowed righteousness upon us, that is, justified us in faith, our lives are meant to mirror this gracious gift of God. Thus, leading an upright life is still crucial to following Jesus.

Paul's letters are filled with ethical advice. Many parts of the letters are devoted exclusively to giving practical advice about many different ethical situations that confronted his communities. One need only look at one of his lists of sins to see the breadth of ethical issues he confronted, under the overarching category of "fleshly" deeds.

> Now the works of the flesh are obvious: fornication, impurity, licentiousness, idolatry, sorcery, enmities, strife, jealousy, anger, quarrels, dissensions, factions, envy, drunkenness, carousing, and things like these. I am warning you, as I warned you before: those who do such things will not inherit the kingdom of God.[3]

People simply don't live as they ought. Thus, Paul called them time and again to return to an upright way of life. He did this primarily by drawing attention to the three "theological" virtues: faith, hope and love. Of course, he also drew attention to other human virtues, like prudence, justice, fortitude, temperance, patience and so on, but the three main virtues that flow from God really provide the central focus of Paul's attention.

What is faith for Paul? It is first and foremost a relationship with God and with Jesus Christ. Faith is both a gift and a response. It comes by God's outreach to us and our free response to this grace-filled offer. Faith is a dynamic bond of trust. Let me illustrate this point with an excerpt from contemporary literature.

Some readers may be familiar with the hugely successful series of short novels by Alexander McCall Smith, entitled *The*

No. 1 Ladies' Detective Agency (also the title of the first book in the series). The heroine is a stout African woman from Botswana, in southern Africa, by the name of Mma Ramotswe. In the course of her many adventures after founding Botswana's first detective agency owned and operated by a woman, Mma Ramotswe imparts a great deal of knowledge about human nature. In one passage, after she has learned of the dishonesty of a local automobile repair shop, she reflects eloquently on the importance of trust in human relationships:

> She was angry; not angry in the loud way in which some people were angry, but quietly, with only pursed lips and a particular look in her eye to show what she was feeling. She had never been able to tolerate dishonesty, which she thought threatened the very heart of relationships between people. If you could not count on other people to mean what they said, or to do what they said they would do, then life could become utterly unpredictable. The fact that we could trust one another made it possible to undertake the simple tasks of life. Everything was based on trust, even day-to-day things like crossing the road—which required trust that the drivers of other cars would be paying attention—to buying the food from a roadside vendor, whom you trusted not to poison you. It was a lesson we learned as children, when our parents threw us up into the sky and thrilled us by letting us drop into their waiting arms. We trusted those arms to be there, and they were.[4]

Saint Paul would approve Mma Ramotswe's wisdom. In fact, for Paul the virtue we call faith is primarily *trust*. As I sometimes say to my students, for Paul, faith is a verb. It is not a static reality. Nor can it be reduced to a set of beliefs or doc-

trines, as important as these are. Faith is primarily a relationship built on trust. One party holds out a hand, the other
grasps it in friendship. The gesture creates a bond. The way
Paul understands it, faith comes from God's reaching out to
us, individually and collectively, and offering us his friendship. As in any honest relationship, the offer is free. We are not
forced to accept it. Indeed, we are free to reject such offers at
any time. But the offer remains, and once accepted, brings us
into a new relationship with God.

Love, of course, is the most important but also the most
challenging of the virtues. Faith leads directly to love. It is the
primary commandment. Paul pays homage to Jesus' teaching
that love of God and neighbor summarizes the whole of the
law of God (the Torah):

> The commandments, "You shall not commit adultery; You
> shall not murder; You shall not steal; You shall not covet";
> and any other commandment, are summed up in this word,
> "Love your neighbor as yourself." Love does no wrong to a
> neighbor; therefore, love is the fulfilling of the law.[5]

More eloquently, in his famous chapter in 1 Corinthians on
the virtue of love, Paul describes how love supersedes all other
gifts in the sphere of human experience. This beautiful chapter is such a gem that I will recommend meditating on it as one
of the spiritual exercises below. Here I will only note one
aspect of it. Paul calls it "a more excellent way" and proceeds
to note some of love's great qualities.

> If I speak in the tongues of mortals and of angels, but do not
> have love, I am a noisy gong or a clanging cymbal. And if I
> have prophetic powers, and understand all mysteries and all

knowledge, and if I have all faith, so as to remove mountains, but do not have love, I am nothing. If I give away all my possessions, and if I hand over my body so that I may boast, but do not have love, I gain nothing. Love is patient; love is kind; love is not envious or boastful or arrogant or rude. It does not insist on its own way; it is not irritable or resentful; it does not rejoice in wrongdoing, but rejoices in the truth. It bears all things, believes all things, hopes all things, endures all things.[6]

These lofty words have been used many times in wedding ceremonies because they call us to a truly higher plane of life. Elsewhere, in fact, Paul uses the marriage bond as a powerful model of the relationship between Christ and the church.[7] Sadly, talking about love is often easier than putting it into action. Marriage is not easy; neither is it easy to put love into action. Just as many marriages in our day "crash and burn" after only a relatively short time, so love often gets eclipsed by selfishness or other distractions.

Now you will probably notice that I seem to have skipped over hope. There is a special reason for this. Hope is truly one of the three theological virtues that Paul treats in his letters. But I am going to save it for the final day of our retreat. It fits neatly with the theme of the last conference and is intimately related to the expectation of God's final victory. So I ask you to be patient, and hope will reappear!

Paul was not innocent of the challenges presented by these three main virtues and a host of others. He knew that although God had bestowed a righteous dignity upon all humankind, frequently people find life easier to live if they revert to tried-and-true selfish ways. It is hard to make faith, hope and love the centerpiece of one's daily routine. It is hard to put the gospel into action.

One way that Paul addressed this situation was to draw attention to what we might call an ethical battle. He sometimes describes getting suited up for this cosmic battle that must be confronted here and now. Using military imagery and the familiar contrast between being those who follow the light rather than the darkness, Paul points out how the virtues help us in our struggle.

> But you, beloved, are not in darkness, for that day to surprise you like a thief; for you are all children of light and children of the day; we are not of the night or of darkness. So then let us not fall asleep as others do, but let us keep awake and be sober; for those who sleep sleep at night, and those who are drunk get drunk at night. But since we belong to the day, let us be sober, and put on the breastplate of faith and love, and for a helmet the hope of salvation. For God has destined us not for wrath but for obtaining salvation through our Lord Jesus Christ, who died for us, so that whether we are awake or asleep we may live with him.[8]

Some of us may find the military imagery a bit troubling. If it is taken too literally, it can lead to problems. We could become overly combative, especially with those whom we perceive not to be living an upright and honest life. This could lead to an arrogant kind of intolerance unbecoming of authentic Christianity.

Paul uses the military imagery not only because it would be familiar with his audience, but also because it makes us look at the ethical life realistically. Life is a struggle. It is fought with little skirmishes and sometimes with big, full-blown battles. Life is like the proverbial dance—two steps forward and one step back. But we must always equip ourselves to advance. The "breastplate" of faith and love help to protect our heart and soul. The "helmet" of hope protects our head; it keeps us rightly oriented toward the future and prevents us from being overwhelmed. Being armed with virtues, rather than armor, equips us for making the right choices and staying on the righteous path that God has already established for us.

Paul would also have us understand a word about what happens when, owing to our human weakness, we fail to live the virtuous life to its fullest extent. Paul knew true failings. But he also knew that, in Christ, any failing can be addressed through God's gift of reconciliation. He writes in 2 Corinthians:

> All this is from God, who reconciled us to himself through Christ, and has given us the ministry of reconciliation; that is, in Christ God was reconciling the world to himself, not counting their trespasses against them, and entrusting the message of reconciliation to us. So we are ambassadors for Christ, since God is making his appeal through us; we entreat you on behalf of Christ, be reconciled to God.[9]

Notice the threefold direction in this passage. God has already reconciled the world to himself in Christ Jesus. But he has also entrusted us to be messengers of reconciliation, to carry it forth in the world. Finally, Paul exhorts the Corinthians strongly: Be reconciled! This triple message is essentially one that reminds us that our ethical failings need never be the final word in our lives. There is always the possibility of reconciliation, because it is one of God's great gifts already given the world through Christ Jesus himself.

Before closing this session, I point out one more aspect of Paul's perspective that influenced his ethical teachings. It concerns his expectation that the end of the world as he knew it was soon to occur. When introducing Paul and his world, I pointed out that apocalyptic thought had influenced Paul. This was partly based upon Jesus' teaching that he would come again to judge the world and to set things right. Paul clearly thought Jesus' return in glory and in judgment would happen soon. As he writes to the Corinthians: "For the present form of this world is passing away."[10] This belief was part of Paul's world and that of the early Christians. This perspective gave Paul a certain urgency in his ethical teaching that likely is lacking in our own time. He preferred that people not change their state in life because the world as they knew it was going to be totally changed, once Jesus had returned.

We no longer live under such constraints, although at times, I wonder whether, with the presence of terrorism, wars, global warming, natural disasters, ethical scandals in business, government and even the church, we can honestly claim that we are immune to dire thoughts of the future of the world! At any rate, the motivation for leading ethically upright lives is not because we fear the end is near, nor because we believe we must act this way to win God's favor. God's gracious favor has already been bestowed upon us permanently in Jesus Christ. We try to lead ethical lives to show the world that there is "a more excellent way." We live upright lives because it is the right thing to do. Goodness is its own reward. This is the kind of perspective I think Paul would heartily approve. As he writes in Ephesians:

For we are what [God] has made us, created in Christ Jesus for good works, which God prepared beforehand to be our way of life.[11]

We should always pray for the strength to lead the virtuous life.

FOR REFLECTION

Quietly examine your own life with regard to the ethical battles that you fight, internally and externally. Where do you think you stand in this fight? Do you ever get discouraged or tempted to give up? What helps you to go on?

Read slowly and thoughtfully 1 Corinthians 13:1–13, Paul's great ode to love. Why is love the greatest virtue? Do you think Paul is being realistic in his description?

How would you describe the ethical dimensions of your life? Are there expressed ethical expectations for your job? Your vocation? How well do you live up to such expectations? Does it matter? Do you think ethical expectations are only a private matter? What effect does an ethically upright life have on others?

Paul frequently called on his readers to imitate him, such as in 1 Corinthians 11:1. What aspects of Paul's life and teachings are most attractive for you to imitate? Are there aspects of Paul's teachings that are difficult to imitate?

CLOSING PRAYER

Lucien Deiss composed the following prayer titled, "I Have Spent My Life, Lord," which I have adapted slightly for the close of this retreat session.[12] It may lead you to reflect on your own strengths and weaknesses in virtue. It might even be considered a kind of examination of conscience.

I have spent my life, Lord,
tuning up my lyre
instead of singing to you.
I'm sorry, Lord.

I have spent my life, Lord,
looking for my own path
instead of walking with you.
I'm sorry, Lord.

I have spent my life, Lord,
begging for love
instead of loving you in my brothers and sisters.
I'm sorry, Lord.

I have spent my life, Lord,
fleeing the night
instead of saying: You are my light.
I'm sorry, Lord.

I have spent my life, Lord,
seeking security
instead of placing my hand in yours.
I'm sorry, Lord.

I have spent my life, Lord,
making resolutions
and not keeping them.
I'm sorry, Lord.

Now, if it is true, Lord,
that you save us
not because of our works

but because of your great mercy,
then we are now ready
to receive your salvation. Amen.

Notes
1. Matthew 18:3–4.
2. 1 Corinthians 3:1–3. Note that he also urges them in 1 Corinthians 14:20 not to think like children.
3. Galatians 5:19–21.
4. Alexander McCall Smith, *The Full Cupboard of Life* (New York: Anchor, 2003), p. 62.
5. Romans 13:9–10. See Jesus' teaching in Mark 12:31, Matthew 22:39 and Luke 10:27. It is curious that Paul leaves out Jesus' instruction about wholehearted love of God, but this may only be due to his concerns he is addressing at the moment, for surely Paul would wholeheartedly agree with the teaching, which was a hallmark of Jewish faith (Deuteronomy 6:4–5).
6. 1 Corinthians 13:1–7.
7. See Ephesians 5:21–33.
8. 1 Thessalonians 5:4–10.
9. 2 Corinthians 5:18–20.
10. 1 Corinthians 7:31.
11. Ephesians 2:10.
12. Lucien Deiss, *Biblical Prayers* (Cincinnati: World Library, 1976), p. 31. The prayer is based upon Ephesians 2:4–10. My only adaptation was to make the expression "brothers" in the third stanza more inclusive.

DAY SEVEN

REJOICING

IN

THE

VICTORY

OF

GOD

COMING TOGETHER IN THE SPIRIT

Many times in my life I have wanted to see justice done, and done quickly. Perhaps it is a streak of self-righteousness that must be purged by God's mercy. Or maybe it is simply a basic human desire to see wrongs righted. Once while driving on a particularly hazardous stretch of mountainous road on the California coast, I was passed by a sleek, speeding sports car. The car was dangerously exceeding the speed limit, and the situation was made all the more treacherous by heavy traffic. Nevertheless, the driver weaved dangerously in and out of traffic, crossing lanes indiscriminately and attempting to pass everyone else on the road. I could tell that it frightened and angered most drivers. I found myself thinking vengefully, where is the CHP (California Highway Patrol) when you most need them?

Lo and behold, a couple of miles down the road, there sat the speeding car. A highway patrolman must have appeared from nowhere and was obviously writing a speeding ticket. As the rest of us drifted by, drivers in car after car tooted their horn and raised a fist in the air. Justice had for once been served!

Was this merely a case of what the Germans call *Schadenfreude*—taking delight in someone else's misfortune? Was it simply relief that a dangerous driver was getting his comeuppance? What makes us desire this swift and proportionate type of justice?

Whatever it is, I know that life doesn't mete out this kind of justice often. Life is simply not that fair. Our deepest desires in this regard are often thwarted. Injustice continues in many situations that are not corrected. Wrongs are not automatically righted in this world. Evil deeds do not always go punished. The unjust often appear to flourish while the righteous languish. Yet I am also conscious that my own desire for swift action can be turned topsy-turvy when it comes to my own wrongdoing.

From this picture one could get discouraged. The perspective of faith, however, calls us to see things differently. This is actually where hope comes into play. Hope is like the future tense of faith. It is forward-looking. We are called to have utter confidence in the ultimate victory of good over evil. God will win the day. Paul, when faced with many challenging and discouraging circumstances in the course of his ministry, called upon this faith perspective or, we might say, this vision of hope. He believed, and he called on his congregations to accept, that in Jesus Christ God's final victory over sin and death is assured. Even in circumstances of apparent defeat, Paul called us to rejoice in this victory. This provides an appropriate focus for our final day of retreat, as we look toward the rest of our life.

OPENING PRAYER

Good and just God, creator and sustainer of all life, I humbly come before you to ask that you give me hope and strength this day to await your final victory over sin and death. I am conscious of my own frailty. I know that I am not perfect in the way that I live your divine law. I also know that sin still dominates so much of our world. We need your salvation. We need your justice. When I am tempted, Lord, to despair in the face of ongoing evil, give me hope. When I am tempted to judge others harshly for their failings, give me patience and the ability to see my own failings. When I am tempted to give up trying to live your laws, give me courage. I place all that I am in your care. I surrender to your will. And I pledge my trust that you will one day bring your just kingdom to fruition. In the name of your risen Son, Jesus, and in the Holy Spirit, I pray now and forever. Amen.

RETREAT SESSION SEVEN

Scripture for Reflection

Rejoice in the Lord always; again I will say, Rejoice! (Philippians 4:4)

What will separate us from the love of Christ? Will tribulation, or distress, or persecution, or famine, or nakedness, or peril, or sword? As it is written,

"For your sake we are being slain all day long;
we are looked upon as sheep to be slaughtered."

No, in all these things we completely prevail through him who loved us. For I am convinced that neither death, nor life, nor angels, nor rulers, nor things present, nor things to come, nor powers, nor height, nor depth, nor any other creature will be able to separate us from the love of God in Christ Jesus our Lord. (Romans 8:35–39; author's translation)

I think almost everyone enjoys a great story of the victory of good over evil or of the righting of an injustice. The popularity in our day of movies with just such a theme illustrates this point. The enormously popular Harry Potter movies, based on the even more successful series of books by J.K. Rowling, offer a rousing picture of this eternal struggle between good and evil, under the theme of magic and wizards. In an earlier era, and happily revived recently in cinema, C.S. Lewis's children's classic, *The Chronicles of Narnia: The Lion, the Witch, and the Wardrobe*, tackled similar themes in an imaginative literary vein. The same could be said for J.R.R. Tolkien's epic *Lord of the Rings* trilogy, which has always been a popular literary work and is now a set of successful movies.

Each of these series addresses the age-old theme of the eternal battle between good and evil by creating a fictional and even mystical universe where the struggle takes place. George Lucas's *Star Wars* movies do the same, from a science fiction vantage point, while even comic book characters like Superman, Batman, Spiderman and Catwoman have been revived in cinema recently to capitalize on our never-ending thirst for stories that hold out the hope of the victory of good over evil.

Paul did not have to invent any imaginary setting to tell his story of the victory of good over evil. Nor did he need a hero who had special magical powers or secret weapons. Instead, Paul simply preached the "gospel" of Jesus Christ. That is, Paul recounted in his letters the ultimate meaning of Jesus' death and resurrection. It was essentially the good news of what God had accomplished in Jesus Christ. He did not do so naïvely. The message is clearly paradoxical. An image of defeat and humiliation—the cross—was shown to be a symbol of victory. Paul's "hero" did not win the victory by a brutal battle and beating the enemy into the ground. He won by surrendering himself, offering himself up for the sake of others and offering the hope of reconciliation. He showed the world that self-sacrificing love conquers all.

Paul squarely faced the ongoing reality of sin and evil, even while he proclaimed that the cross and resurrection of Jesus had established God's victory. The Letter to the Romans contains the most extensive and coherent treatment of this issue, and we might reflect on it in this final retreat conference.

Paul lays out his understanding of the situation in chapters one to three of Romans. His argument goes something like this: The world, as defined in his day, constituted a dual reality. Jews viewed it from their perspective as God's chosen people. They were Jews; everyone else was gentile. The Greeks, however, had their own perspective, just as dualistic. They divided the world into two camps: either Greek or barbarian. This tendency to divide the world in two, us and them, perhaps is just part of the human condition. In any case, Paul attacks such a dualistic view, especially when it leads to self-righteousness and the implication that one human worldview is better than another.

Paul goes on to point out that while both Jews and Greeks (gentiles) had advantages that should have helped them to know right from wrong, they both also harbored a lot of evil. The Jews had the Law (Torah), while the Greeks had wisdom (philosophy). Both should have helped them to see the truth. At one point, Paul catalogues the extensive sins of the Greek world.

> They were filled with every kind of wickedness, evil, covetousness, malice. Full of envy, murder, strife, deceit, craftiness, they are gossips, slanderers, God-haters, insolent, haughty, boastful, inventors of evil, rebellious toward parents, foolish, faithless, heartless, ruthless. They know God's decree, that those who practice such things deserve to die— yet they not only do them but even applaud others who practice them.[1]

This is pretty damning evidence. One could almost imagine the Jewish members of the community smirking and thinking to themselves: "We're not like that!"

But Paul does not give them any chance for self-commendation. For he immediately turns to an analysis of the Jewish world and its faults. They, who have received God's Law through Moses, and who should thus know better, are actually just as ingrained with sin and failure as the gentiles. He warns them sternly not to pass judgment on others. (Remember the saying, "people who live in glass houses should not throw stones"?)

> Therefore you have no excuse, whoever you are, when you judge others; for in passing judgment on another you condemn yourself, because you, the judge, are doing the very same things. You say, "We know that God's judgment on those who do such things is in accordance with truth." Do you imagine, whoever you are, that when you judge those who do such things and yet do them yourself, you will escape the judgment of God? Or do you despise the riches

of his kindness and forbearance and patience? Do you not realize that God's kindness is meant to lead you to repentance? But by your hard and impenitent heart you are storing up wrath for yourself on the day of wrath, when God's righteous judgment will be revealed. For he will repay according to each one's deeds: to those who by patiently doing good seek for glory and honor and immortality, he will give eternal life; while for those who are self-seeking and who obey not the truth but wickedness, there will be wrath and fury. There will be anguish and distress for everyone who does evil, the Jew first and also the Greek, but glory and honor and peace for everyone who does good, the Jew first and also the Greek. For God shows no partiality.[2]

With these stinging words, Paul reminds the Jewish members of the community that they should be careful about considering themselves "a guide to the blind and a light to those who are in darkness."[3] God is not partial and shows no favorites. The reality, from Paul's analysis, was that both the Jewish and gentile worlds needed salvation. Both the Jews and the Greeks had failed to live properly as God's creatures, created in God's own image. Neither had won its victory over evil. For all humanity is in need of God's salvation.

This is precisely where Jesus Christ enters the picture for Paul. If his analysis is accurate, and the evidence in daily life in our day would indicate that it is, then he rightly draws attention to the universal need for salvation. We humans cannot win the battle against evil on our own. Our human tendency—actually, our natural inclination to sin—exercises a power over us that is difficult to resist. Just when we think we have made it, or when we think we have won our victory, that is often when our failings catch up to us. Slippage happens: the alcoholic who abandons the twelve-step process, the husband who once more neglects his wife or children, the businessperson who cheats a customer or cannot resist fudging on taxes, the adulterer who cannot resist one more liaison. Sin abounds, says Paul, but grace abounds all the more.[4]

But Paul understands just how big a challenge it can be to remain hopeful in the midst of the ongoing evidence of sin. In a famous passage in Romans, Paul lays out what might be his personal predicament, but which can also be seen as the universal human condition as it is experienced apart from Christ. He complains that although he knows what good is required to be done, he fails so often to do it.

> I do not understand my own actions. For I do not do what I want, but I do the very thing I hate. ...But in fact it is no longer I that do it, but sin that dwells within me. For I know that nothing good dwells within me, that is, in my flesh. I can will what is right, but I cannot do it. For I do not do the good I want, but the evil I do not want is what I do. Now if I do what I do not want, it is no longer I that do it, but sin that dwells within me. So I find it to be a law that when I want to do what is good, evil lies close at hand. For I delight in the law of God in my inmost self, but I see in my members another law at war with the law of my mind, making me captive to the law of sin that dwells in my members. Wretched man that I am! Who will rescue me from this body of death?[5]

This passage explains the human dilemma in the absence of Christ so clearly. Deep down, we know what is right. But we do not have the strength to accomplish it. Putting the right into action, especially in the face of the world's allurements, is difficult to do. Only when we live in Christ can we see our way through this muddled situation.

So what is our plight? Are we doomed to wallow in our sinfulness? Are we never to achieve an ultimate victory?

This is where Paul becomes his most creative. He reflects in depth on the ultimate meaning of Jesus' coming into the world and the effect of his death and resurrection. If we were doomed only to be creatures of our human nature, limited sons and daughters of Adam and Eve, we would indeed have little hope. But there is a "new Adam," says Paul, who now gives all creation a new chance.[6] Of course, he is speaking of Jesus Christ. In him, all people now have the possibility of defeating evil, sin and death once and for all. He has made us adopted children of God. His victory by the cross and Resurrection is our doorway to new life. "There is therefore now no condemnation for those who are in Christ Jesus."[7] In Jesus Christ, God provides the victory that would otherwise elude us.

This is where the virtue of hope arrives on the scene. I delayed consideration of this theological virtue until here because it belongs with confidence in God's victory.

In a remarkable passage in Romans, Paul points out how hope emerges from a series of interrelated events caused by God's graciousness.

> Therefore, since we are justified by faith, we have peace with God through our Lord Jesus Christ, through whom we have obtained access to this grace in which we stand; and we boast in our hope of sharing the glory of God. And not only that, but we also boast in our sufferings, knowing that suffering produces endurance, and endurance produces

character, and character produces hope, and hope does not disappoint us, because God's love has been poured into our hearts through the Holy Spirit that has been given to us.[8]

Basically, Paul shows us a series of grace-filled realities that lead to hope. We might say, hope comes from God and leads us back to God, in confidence. Elsewhere Paul writes to his colleague Timothy that hope is rooted in confidence in God: "...we have our hope set on the living God, who is the Savior of all people, especially of those who believe."[9] And he reminds the Romans: "For in hope we were saved. Now hope that is seen is not hope. For who hopes for what is seen? But if we hope for what we do not see, we wait for it with patience."[10]

Hope is always forward-looking, anticipating the fulfillment of what has been promised. At times Paul has to exhort his communities never to lose hope, despite the temptation to do so in light of life's struggles. The Thessalonians were clearly such a community. Some members had lost hope because loved ones had died. They became fearful that these people would miss out on the final day of God's victory. So Paul reminds them:

> For since we believe that Jesus died and rose again, even so, through Jesus, God will bring with him those who have died. For this we declare to you by the word of the Lord, that we who are alive, who are left until the coming of the Lord, will by no means precede those who have died.... Therefore encourage one another with these words.[11]

This is why, by the way, when Paul speaks to the Thessalonians about the three theological virtues, hope is listed last, i.e., the place of emphasis. He reminds them of the need to live in faith, love and hope.[12] In their case, hope was the virtue that got the least attention. Paul comforts and exhorts them in their predicament in order to re-enliven their hope. They had already demonstrated their faith and their love, but they needed to rekindle their hope. Hope is faith that is oriented to the future in confidence. It does not yield to appearances in this world. Nor is it weakened by seeming detours or delays in God's plan of salvation.

I cannot stress too much the importance of Paul's belief in the resurrection for his confidence in God's final triumph. The resurrection of Jesus was a preliminary to our own resurrection. Paul considers Jesus the "first fruits" of this hope. He writes in 1 Corinthians:

> But in fact Christ has been raised from the dead, the first fruits of those who have died. For since death came through a human being, the resurrection of the dead has also come through a human being; for as all die in Adam, so all will be made alive in Christ. But each in his own order: Christ the first fruits, then at his coming those who belong to Christ. Then comes the end, when he hands over the kingdom to God the Father, after he has destroyed every ruler and every authority and power. For he must reign until he has put all his enemies under his feet. The last enemy to be destroyed is death. For "God has put all things in subjection under his feet." ...When all things are subjected to him, then the Son himself will also be subjected to the one who put all things in subjection under him, so that God may be all in all.[13]

Just as Jesus conquered death by the Resurrection, so we all will participate in the final victory when the dead are raised into glory.

This was one of the most difficult messages to get across in Paul's day, believe it or not. The reason is that the notion of the resurrection seemed absurd. Who ever heard of anyone rising from the dead? The Acts of the Apostles records such a reaction to Paul's preaching in Athens: "When they heard of the resurrection of the dead, some scoffed...." [14]

But the resurrection is indeed the foundation of our Christian faith. Does it make sense in worldly terms? No. Yet Paul insists, "If there is no resurrection of the dead, then Christ has not been raised; and if Christ has not been raised, then our proclamation has been in vain and your faith has been in vain." [15] We also profess this faith in the creed, when we say we believe in the resurrection of the dead and life everlasting. This is the message we proclaim every time we gather to say farewell to someone we love who has died. It is an act of faith and an act of hope. Our confidence in the resurrection is an act of trust that God will ultimately be victorious over all that is finite. Sin and death will no longer hold sway over us.

Paul's most eloquent summary of his confidence in God's ultimate victory is found in Romans 8. These words bring this conference to an appropriate close. He writes forcefully:

We know that all things work together for good for those who love God, who are called according to his purpose. For those whom he foreknew he also predestined to be conformed to the image of his Son, in order that he might be the firstborn within a large family. And those whom he predestined he also called; and those whom he called he also justified; and those whom he justified he also glorified. What then are we to say about these things? If God is for us, who is against us? He who did not withhold his own Son, but gave him up for all of us, will he not with him also give us everything else? Who will bring any charge against God's elect? It is God who justifies. Who is to condemn? It is Christ Jesus, who died, yes, who was raised, who is at the right hand of God, who indeed intercedes for us. Who will separate us from the love of Christ? Will hardship, or distress, or persecution, or famine, or nakedness, or peril, or sword? As it is written,

> "For your sake we are being killed all day long;
> we are accounted as sheep to be slaughtered."

No, in all these things we are more than conquerors through him who loved us. For I am convinced that neither death, nor life, nor angels, nor rulers, nor things present, nor things to come, nor powers, nor height, nor depth, nor anything else in all creation, will be able to separate us from the love of God in Christ Jesus our Lord.[16]

So this is our reason for confidence, for hope and even for rejoicing in the midst of life's daily struggles. In fact, hope is inevitably accompanied by joy. This is not a human joy, in the sense of something that gives us pleasure for a time, or makes us feel good or happy, or causes us to smile or laugh.

Christian joy is a deeply felt reality of well-being. It is rooted in the confidence that God will help us surmount any difficulty and will provide the victory we so desire. That is why Paul can so emphasize joy even in the letters he writes from prison, especially Philippians. He has set his hope on Jesus, and joy has filled him because of it. In one of his prayerful wishes, he writes to the Romans about his desire that they approach their faith in this manner: "May the God of hope fill you with all joy and peace in believing, so that you may abound in hope by the power of the Holy Spirit."[17]

In the end, the melding of hope and joy and victory puts us in touch with the mystery that is God. Although it is a mystery, God's salvation will finally have its desired effect. The victory is not ours, really. It is God's. But God chooses to share it with us, and he invites all to participate in this salvation. This is great cause for rejoicing, as we begin to bring our retreat to a close.

FOR REFLECTION

Read Psalm 18:2–3: "The LORD is my rock, my fortress, and my deliverer, / my God, my rock in whom I take refuge, / my shield, and the horn of my salvation, my stronghold. / I call upon the LORD who is worthy to be praised, / so I shall be saved from my enemies." The psalmist uses strong imagery to express confidence in God. Does this imagery express your own experience of confidence in God? Can you use your own words to give thanks for God's care over you?

Read Romans 8:38–39 again. What kinds of "present things," "future things," "powers" or "any other creature" threaten your life? Can you express the same confidence as Paul that none of these obstacles will prevent you from experiencing the loving salvation of God?

Take time to dwell on the image of the resurrection of Jesus. If you have time, read all of 1 Corinthians 15, Paul's longest reflection on the resurrection. What do you find comforting in this belief? Can you identify any anxieties associated with it? How strong is your personal conviction that God's victory over sin and death will win out in the end?

Read 1 Thessalonians 4:13–18. Paul writes about not losing hope that those who "have fallen asleep" will rise on the last day. Although the imagery of the actual event of Christ's coming in glory in the last days is not meant to be taken literally, the passage is intended to sustain hope in the resurrection. Do you find anything in the passage consoling? Does it stretch one's imagination? What message of hope do you find there?

CLOSING PRAYER

Lord of the universe, your power is beyond all comprehension. I can scarcely fathom how your victory will look on that day when your kingdom comes. Yet I profess my faith in you because of the example of your own Son, Jesus. He surrendered himself to your will, and you vindicated him in the resurrection. On that day the light truly overcame the darkness. New life won out over the power of death. And you restored hope to the world. Never let my confidence be shaken by the terrible events that sometimes happen around me. Come, Lord, and accomplish your victory. Gather all into your bosom. In his name, who is risen Lord, and in your Holy Spirit, I pray. Amen.

Notes
1. Romans 1:29–31.
2. Romans 2:1–11.
3. Romans 2:19.
4. See Romans 5:20.
5. Romans 7:15, 17–24.
6. See Romans 5:14 and 1 Corinthians 15:22. For a short summary of Paul's understanding of Christ as the "new Adam," see Ronald D. Witherup, *101 Questions & Answers on Paul* (Mahwah, N.J.: Paulist, 2003), pp. 122–124.
7. Romans 8:1.
8. Romans 5:1–5.
9. 1 Timothy 4:10.

10. Romans 8:24-25.
11. 1 Thessalonians 4:14-15, 18.
12. See 1 Thessalonians 1:3; 5:8.
13. 1 Corinthians 15:20-28.
14. Acts 17:32a.
15. 1 Corinthians 15:13-15.
16. Romans 8:28-39.
17. Romans 15:13.

SO WE COME TO THE LAST FEW THOUGHTS ON OUR retreat, ready to move ahead on our spiritual journey. Before taking a glance into the future, it may be useful to rehearse briefly what we have encountered on our retreat with the remarkable "apostle to the Gentiles."

With Paul we have looked at the following seven aspects of the spiritual life:

- in Christ Jesus, we have been invited to become a new creation;
- we are each called by name, justified, saved by grace and destined for glory;
- we are urged to embrace the cross as part of our spiritual journey;
- we are invited to live in the Holy Spirit, who accompanies us on our journey of faith;
- we are asked to pray without ceasing;
- we are expected to lead a virtuous life, especially putting into practice faith, hope and love;
- we are encouraged to rejoice always, knowing that God promises the ultimate victory over sin and death.

If we have not plumbed all the depths of Paul's spiritual vision, we have made a very good beginning on this retreat. Paul would be the first to encourage and exhort us to take the next steps toward spiritual wholeness. If you have discovered nothing else on this retreat, I hope that you at least have found out what a treasure we have in the letters of Paul. Befriending him can take you much further on the spiritual journey than you probably ever imagined.

A retreat is like an oasis in the desert. It provides an opportunity for refreshment and renewal, but in itself it is not the end of the journey. A retreat supplies spiritual energy to go on and to confront the challenges that await us day in and day out. How do we best harness this energy to help sustain us on the journey of life?

If we could literally ask our retreat director, Paul the apostle, what he would recommend, I think he would have at least three pieces of advice.

First, to return to the theme of our retreat, Paul would want us to acknowledge the "fragile treasure" that we have been given in the spiritual life. The spiritual journey we are on is lived in the here and now and is a call to conversion. It is experienced in flesh and blood. It is not something limited to retreat experiences and spiritual "highs." It does not suddenly arrive when the kingdom of God does. It is lived in the peaks and valleys of ordinary life. Although God has given us the power to become his children, we are always in the process of being molded more and more into the image of his divine Son, Jesus Christ, with the assistance of the Holy Spirit.

Paul knew that the spiritual journey was fraught with many obstacles. It is a fragile enterprise. It can be derailed at any time, especially when we lose sight of the larger goal—the kingdom of God. Life's petty concerns, which can at times seem like insurmountable mountains, can interfere with the well-being God wishes us to have. Yet a solid spiritual life is within our reach. Paul would urge us to remain steadfast in our resolve to deepen our relationship with God. Just as he encouraged his own communities, he says to us now: Stay firm in your faith; don't let setbacks discourage you; don't ever give up! Rejoice, pray, give thanks and move on, resolve to do better and trust that God will supply whatever is lacking in your resolve to make progress. As he writes to his beloved Thessalonians:

> And we urge you, beloved, to admonish the idlers, encourage the fainthearted, help the weak, be patient with all of them. See that none of you repays evil for evil, but always seek to do good to one another and to all. Rejoice always, pray without ceasing, give thanks in all circumstances; for this is the will of God in Christ Jesus for you. Do not quench the Spirit. Do not despise the words of prophets, but test everything; hold fast to what is good; abstain from every form of evil. May the God of peace himself sanctify you entirely; and may your spirit and soul and body be kept sound and blameless at the coming of our Lord Jesus Christ.[1]

Second, Paul would want us to immerse ourselves in our respective communities of faith. Just as he fostered new life in the communities that he founded and served, he would want us to experience the profound support that comes from a community rooted in faith, built upon love and unwavering in hope. Paul challenged his readers to honor the communal dimension of their salvation. They were called to recognize the individual gifts that made up the community, but to acknowledge as well that the same Spirit brought these gifts into being. When we are refreshed individually by a retreat experience, our recharged spiritual "batteries" can help animate those around us. When we see things afresh, our vision can positively affect the vision of others. When we gain courage to confront our ordinary life, we can encourage others to do likewise.

I think Paul would make a third recommendation as well. It concerns using sacred Scripture for personal spiritual growth. He was imbued with the sacred Scriptures we now call the Old Testament. Reading his letters reveals just how influential these writings were in his life. He lived and breathed them. He not only reflected on them, but he also memorized some of them. Through them he came to know more of the mystery of God and God's plan for the world. He was a master at interpreting them in new circumstances. He would want us always to keep the sacred Scriptures front and center in our spiritual lives.

Now, some two thousand years removed from Paul, he would be astonished to think that his own letters have become sacred writings, part of what we now call the New Testament. Although he envisioned that his letters might (and should) be read widely among his own communities,[2] he never thought of them as Scripture. They were letters, after all. They were simple means of staying in touch with those dearest to him in faith. Yet Scripture is what they are.

Paul's letters have become the Word of God to faith communities for all generations to come. Consequently, I think he would be happy if we would continue to read his letters and reflect on them as we go about our daily lives. In the course of this retreat, we have only touched on some of the more prominent spiritual themes of Paul. Reading his letters would provide a more thorough view of the profound teachings that he offers the church today.

Thus, I encourage you to continue to read Paul's letters themselves and to let them speak to you directly. Don't let yourself be intimidated by them. There is no real substitute for the direct encounter with the Word of God. I make one recommendation, however. It is easier to understand Paul if readers begin with his more "practical" letters (e.g., 1 and 2 Corinthians, 1 Thessalonians, Philippians) before engaging the more theologically challenging ones (e.g., Romans, Galatians). Whatever choice you make, though, remember that Paul can always enrich your life. If occasionally you come away puzzled by what he says, know that you are not the first, nor will you be the last. But never let that deter you from reading his letters. Trust that the Holy Spirit will supply whatever is lacking in your own understanding.

Finally, retreats often lead to insights that one might want to pursue later in a more detailed way. As an aid to that desire, this book provides a short, annotated list of resources that can help readers deepen their acquaintance with Paul. These include resources for different levels of engagement. Readers may choose what will be of most benefit at a given time and perhaps choose more sophisticated works as their thirst for knowledge deepens. In any case, readers will benefit from the hands of experts who have studied Paul's writings in depth and can lead the way to ever-deepening insights.

To give Paul the last word on this retreat, we conclude with his own words to his beloved Thessalonians. His prayer for them is a prayer appropriate for each of us on this retreat. It is also, dear reader, my prayer for you:

> May the God of peace himself sanctify you entirely; and may your spirit and soul and body be kept sound and blameless at the coming of our Lord Jesus Christ. The one who calls you is faithful, and he will do this.[3]

Notes
1. 1 Thessalonians 5:14–23.
2. See 1 Thessalonians 5:27 and Colossians 4:16.
3. 1 Thessalonians 5:23–24.

DEEPENING YOUR ACQUAINTANCE

Books

Brown, Raymond E. *An Introduction to the New Testament.* New York: Doubleday, 1997, "Part III: The Pauline Letters," pp. 407–680. A masterful summary of the content and major interpretational issues of Paul's letters by one of the leading Roman Catholic scholars of the twentieth century. Although scholarly, the clarity of thought and expression can appeal to a broad audience.

Decaux, Alain. *Paul, Least of the Apostles: The Story of the Most Unlikely Witness to Christ.* Boston: Pauline, 2006. A popular "biography" of the apostle intended for the average reader, written by a journalist and historian and translated from the original French edition. The book contains some beautiful color photographs of archaeological sites and artistic renderings of Paul.

Fitzmyer, Joseph A. *Spiritual Exercises Based Upon Paul's Epistle to the Romans.* Grand Rapids: Eerdmans, 2004. A sophisticated interlinking of the Ignatian method of retreats with Paul's Letter to the Romans. The format could be used on eight-day directed retreats in conjunction with the *Spiritual Exercises* of Saint Ignatius of Loyola. For more advanced readers.

Gorman, Michael J. *Apostle of the Crucified Lord: A Theological Introduction to Paul and His Letters.* Grand Rapids: Eerdmans, 2004. A thorough, college- or seminary-level textbook introduction to Paul and his theology. For more advanced readers.

Hooker, Morna D. *Paul: A Short Introduction.* Oxford: OneWorld, 2003. A brief, readable summary of basic information on Paul and his letters. For average readers.

Murphy-O'Connor, Jerome. *Paul: His Story.* Oxford: Oxford University Press, 2004. A delightful reconstruction of Paul's life and letters by one who is familiar with both the archaeological and theological data. Readers should note, however, that the author sometimes makes bold hypothetical assertions that many scholars would question.

Soards, Marion L. *The Apostle Paul: An Introduction to His Writings and Teaching.* Mahwah, N.J.: Paulist, 1986. A fine, succinct overview of each letter in the Pauline corpus. For average readers.

Thomas, Carolyn, S.C.N. *Reading the Letters of Saint Paul: Study, Reflection and Prayer.* Mahwah, N.J.: Paulist, 2002. A book for the average reader interested in reflecting more deeply on the message of Paul's writings for personal inspiration and prayer.

Tobin, Thomas. *The Spirituality of Paul.* Wilmington, Del.: Michael Glazier, 1991. A good, general introduction to the spiritual themes in Paul's letters. For the average reader.

Wenham, David. *Paul and Jesus: The True Story.* Grand Rapids: Eerdmans, 2002. A readable but scholarly summary of Paul's teachings in relation to those of Jesus. For more advanced readers.

Witherup, Ronald D. *101 Questions & Answers on Paul.* Mahwah, N.J.: Paulist Press, 2003. Using the simple question-and-answer format of the series, this book introduces average readers to many basic issues in the study of Paul and his letters.

Media

DeSales Catholic Adult Education Program, Series 4: The Writings of Saint Paul. Cincinnati: St. Anthony Messenger Press, 1989. A series of eight one-hour videos on various aspects of Paul and his letters. Intended for group study, the set includes a facilitator's guide pamphlet. Participant manuals can be purchased separately.

Paul the Apostle. The Bible Collection; New York: Good Times, 2000. An imaginative and engaging three-hour recreation of Paul's ministry in DVD format, primarily based upon the Acts of the Apostles. Available through Christian Book Distributors, Peabody, Massachusetts.

Rohr, Richard. *Great Themes in Paul: Life as Participation.* Audiotapes or CDs; Cincinnati: St. Anthony Messenger Press, 2002. A bestselling presentation of Paul's greatest teachings by a popular speaker, intended for a general audience.

For those who are Internet-savvy, the Web site "Journeys of Paul" maintained by Professor Craig Koester of Luther Seminary in Saint Paul, Minnesota, offers a convenient and reliable summary of Paul's missionary journeys, accompanied by beautiful photographs. It is available at: luthersem.edu/ckoester/Paul/Main.htm.